New Perspectives on Indian Writing

In the same series

Indian Literature Today, 2 vols.
R.K. Dhawan, ed.

Recent Indian Fiction
R.S. Pathak, ed.

Five Indian Novelists
V.V.N. Rajendra Prasad

Major Indian Novelists
K. Venkata Reddy

Indian Women Novelists, Set I (Vols. I-V); Set II (Vol.VI-XI)
R.K. Dhawan, ed.

The Novels of Mulk Raj Anand
R.K. Dhawan, ed.

The Novels of Arun Joshi
R.K. Dhawan, ed.

The Novels of Salman Rushdie
G.R. Taneja and R.K. Dhawan, ed.

The Novels of Raja Rao
Esha Dey

The Novels of Bhabani Bhattacharya
Balram Sorot

The Novels of Anita Desai
Usha Bande

Nayantara Sahgal and Doris Lessing: A Feminist Study in Comparison
Neena Arora

The Novels of Shashi Deshpande
Sarabjit K. Sandhu

Comparative Perspectives on Indian Literature
A. Ramakrishna Rao, ed.

Studies in Indian Writing in English
P. Bayapa Reddy

The Novels of Manohar Malgonkar
M. Rajagopalachari

Virginia Woolf and Anita Desai: A Comparative Study
Asha Kanwar

The Novels of Kamala Markandaya and Ruth Jhabvala
Rekha Jha

The World of Malgudi: A Study of R.K. Narayan's Novels
A. Hariprasanna

New Perspectives on Indian Writing

Edited by

V.L.V.N. Narendra Kumar

PRESTIGE

Published by
Prestige Books
3/28, East Patel Nagar
New Delhi 110 008

ISBN: 81-7551-027-7

1997

Photo Typesetting by
Pivot Computers
Delhi 110 006
Ph. 2934490

Printed at
Mehra Offset Press
New Delhi 110 002

CONTENTS

IV

For
My Brother
Kushal Ram

Preface

The idea to bring out an anthology of critical essays on Indian writing in English originated when our Department conducted a seminar on this subject in February 1996. The original plan was to include the papers of students who participated in the seminar. As the University examinations were fast approaching, it was not possible to bring the students together after the seminar for discussions and revision of papers. Hence the inability to include their papers in this volume. However, in the appendix, I gave details of the proceedings of our seminar.

The scholars I solicited papers from, responded enthusiastically to my call. I am indebted to them.

I thank the Management of Andhra Loyola College, Vijayawada for encouraging me at every stage of this enterprise.

Finally a word of thanks to Prestige Books, New Delhi for bringing out the book so well.

Andhra Loyola College
Vijayawada

VLVN NARENDRA KUMAR

Acknowledgements

The Editor wishes to thank the following scholars whose articles are reprinted in this anthology with kind permission:

Dr. Ranga Rao for his article "Contemplative Tiger" which was originally published in *London Magazine* in June/July 1990.

Dr. C.N. Srinath for his paper on Arun Joshi's *The Apprentice* which appeared first in *Consiglio Nazionale Delle Ricerche*, an Italian journal.

Dr. Ragini Ramachandra for her paper on Vikram Seth's *The Golden Gate* which was presented at a seminar at Dhvanyaloka.

Introduction

V.L.V.N. NARENDRA KUMAR

> Our method of expression therefore has to be a dialect which will some day prove to be as distinctive and colourful as the Irish or the American. Time aione will justify it.
>
> Raja Rao, Foreword to *Kanthapura*

The fruition of Indian writing in English is beyond doubt now. The Herculean task of giving this 'new' literature a tangible identity was performed by Srinivasa Iyengar, a prototype in Indian English literary criticism. English became an 'Indian' language in the post-colonial context. Many an Indian creative writer took the advice of Gosse to Sarojini. Consequently, Indian writing in English acquired a distinct Indian character. Narayan's fiction, Ramanujan's poetry and Karnad's plays bear testimony to the stature Indian English literature attained.

To infer that Indian English poetry has arrived is to emphasise the obvious. The seeds of grandeur were sown in the nineteenth century by Derozio and Toru. Sarojini Naidu was the last romantic whose verse is strikingly reminiscent of the best work of Keats and Shelley. The works of Tagore and Sri Aurobindo are the expressions of spiritual life of India.

Ezekiel's is a major voice in Indian English poetry today. Albeit a 'natural outsider,' he has not withdrawn from India. A poet who 'waits for words,' he has become an integral part of the Indian environment. For him, poetry is a means to self-therapy and the bulk of poetry he published so far, reflects the maturity he achieved since the publication of *A Time to Change* in 1952. Like Donne and other metaphysical poets, Ezekiel celebrates sex and morality in his poetry. His poetry is characterized by earthiness and 'homespun wisdom.'

Keki Daruwalla holds a unique position in Indian English poetry. A Zoroastrian, he views poetry as an aid in coming to terms with one's interior world. His perspective is that of an exile; he is a poet who can 'smell violence in the air.' His vocation perhaps toughened him so much that his tone often becomes bitter and satiric. His "Routine" is a case in point.

Ramanujan is a neo-modernist whose vision is ironic. In him, East and West do not clash but complement each other. An orthodox Hindu who stayed in the west too long, he draws freely on Indian legends and folklore. Family is at the centre of his scheme of things. In poems like "Small-Scale Reflections on a Great House" and "Of Mothers and Other Things," the ethos pervading is characteristically Indian.

Kamala Das is the first authentic woman poet who has carved out a special niche for herself in Indian English poetry. Her poetry is by and large autobiographical and is cast in the confessional mode. Her poem "An Introduction" is a stern rejoinder to the detractors of Indian English literature. Her words,

> The language I speak
> Become mine, its distortions, its queernesses
> All mine, mine alone. It is half English, half Indian,
> Funny perhaps, but it is honest,
> It is as human as I am human,
> don't you see?

are typical of an individualist. In her poetry is perceptible a quest for love and fulfilment in life. Thoroughly disillusioned, she seeks a meaningful alternative to the traditional man-woman relationship. Her poetry registers the protest against the ambivalence in the Indian value system.

Jawaharlal Nehru was the blue-blooded son of Mother India whose contribution to Indian writing in English is no less substantial. His *Discovery of India* and *Glimpses of World History* are epics in prose which reflect his intellectual stamina. *Autobiography* is the record of his inner life, the story of transformation of an aristocrat into a fierce patriot. Nehru's language is immaculate and he "out-Britishes" the British in the use of English idiom.

A pacifist through and through, Radhakrishnan was India's answer to Russell. His life was an attempt to narrow the East-West divide. He strove throughout his life to interpret India for the west, a task commenced by Swami Vivekananda. His life was a spiritual adventure. A votary of peace and social justice, he regarded war as an evil which would destroy the social fabric of the world. But unlike Russell, he preferred a diligent adherence to tradition. He laid emphasis on inner transformation and power of knowledge.

Radhakrishnan's views as a thinker are profound and original. He highlights the need for positive living in works like *The Hindu View of Life*. Aware of the limitations of science, he sought an 'experiential religion' which would usher in harmony and stability. His essay *Kalki* is an elegy in prose in which he voices his concern over the deteriorating conditions in various spheres of life viz., religion, family, politics, economic relations and international relations.

The greatest intellect of our age, Nirad C. Chaudhuri continues to be an enigma in Indian writing in English. A writer at loggerheads with the sterile Indian milieu, his accounts of India and Indian life are ruthlessly realistic and down to earth. He is an outsider in his own land whose provocative inferences annoyed the mediocre and the neo-patriotic Indians. The extreme stance he strikes becomes a moral necessity for him. *The Continent of Circe* is a scathing indictment of the predominantly Hindu society whereas his 'Discovery of India' in England is a disturbing experience for the reader.

Indian drama in English is an endangered genre. Today novel is the most popular form and consequently, drama becomes a victim of neglect.

Tagore's *Chandalika, Sacrifice* and *Mukta-Dhara* have great contemporaneous relevance. *Chandalika* is a play of education, a tragedy of self-indulgence. The movement of Prakriti's mind from submission to assertion and the eventual realization of her limitations are depicted convincingly. *Mukta-Dhara* is a thesis play in which Abhijit's quest is for freedom. In liberating the river, he discovers himself. The two selves—inner and outer—merge at the end. *Sacrifice* highlights the evil effects of the barbarous custom of animal sacrifice. In his plays, Tagore does not merely raise questions; he seeks answers which have ecumenical validity.

Girish Karnad is a multifaceted personality whose plays have contact with the 'living stage.' His *Yayati* is a re-interpretation of a well-known Indian myth. The motif of this play is the existential dilemma of a hungry soul whose aspiration for completeness remains unrealised. In *Hayavadana* Karnad brings out the ambiguous nature of human personality. This play too deals with a 'search for completeness.' *Tughlaq* is a historical play. Karnad's triumph lies in laying bare the anguished soul of Tughlaq, a bundle of contradictions. His portrayal of this dreamer is sympathetic to a high degree.

Vijay Tendulkar is another major Indian dramatist in English in whose plays a 'clash of wills' becomes central. He was profoundly influenced by Ionesco. *Silence!The Court is in Session* is an Absurdist play. What starts as a game turns into a hunt with Benare at the receiving end. She is denied basic human needs—love and sympathy. She is victimized whereas Prof. Damle, the man who impregnates her, goes scotfree. The verdict of the 'Court' comes as no surprise. Benare's confession at the end of the mock-trial strikes the keynote:

> Life is a poisonous snake that bites itself. Life is betrayal. Life is fraud. Life is a drug. Life is a drudgery. Life is a something that's nothing—or a nothing that's something. Milord, life is a very dreadful thing. Life must be hanged. *Na jeevan jeevana-marhati.* Life is not worthy of life. Hold an enquiry against life.

Silence! The Court is in Session centrestages the indifference of the society to the suffering of individuals.

Anand, Narayan and Raja Rao shaped the destiny of Indian English fiction. Anand's commitment to the cause of the exploited in our society is genuine and total. A born rebel, he puts himself into his protagonists who reject the pro-haves system. His *Untouchable* is the first authentic Dalit novel in English. The theory that only literature written by Dalits could be regarded as Dalit literature is hardly tenable. Dalit sensibility operates at both the levels of the novel—narrative and linguistic. Anand effectively employs the Dalit idiom which lends authenticity to the narrative. Narayan's fiction highlights the dilemma of average men and women of India. The world of Malgudi is not different from the world we are familiar with. The triumph of his fiction is due to the reader's identification with the characters of Narayan like Margayya, Jagan, Natraj, Chandran and Sriram.

Raja Rao's preoccupations are essentially metaphysical. He is a writer as *Upasaka* for whom the word is the thing. He regards God as the fixed spiritual point of reference. *Kanthapura*, his first novel, is an artistic success. The narrative is a subtle blend of Indian ethos and English expression. Ramaswami's search is not for God but for a guru who can show him the path of liberation. *The Chessmaster and His Moves*, Raja Rao's latest work, is repetitive and does not contribute much to Indian English novel in any conceivable way.

Shashi Tharoor, Vikram Seth, Amitav Ghosh and Upamanyu Chatterjee are our University Wits. Nurtured in the St. Stephen's milieu, they have given a new direction to Indian English fiction. They are the worthy successors to Anand, Narayan and Raja Rao. What characterizes their fiction is technical innovativeness (a trend set by Rushdie with his *Midnight's Children*) and linguistic virtuosity.

Shashi Tharoor's fiction is infused with "the greatness" of India's cultural heritage, of the *Mahabharata*. His works are didactic ones masquerading as entertainments. He is a novelist who entertains in order to edify. In *The Great Indian Novel*, he sets out 'to explore what has made India and nearly unmade it, and about the nature of truth, in life as in fiction, in tradition as in history.' His novels seek to tell a story of India in an essentially Indian voice.

Amitav Ghosh is another promising novelist who began to write in the late eighties. *The Shadow Lines* is a three-generational saga involving East and West. The narrative depicts the impact of history on ordinary lives. Memory becomes the key determinant in the evolution of the Boy's consciousness. The cities, Calcutta, London and Dhaka are separated by imaginary or 'shadow' lines, but 'each city was the inverted image of the other.' Ghosh's *The Circle of Reason* is in the picaresque mode.

Upamanyu Chatterjee was catapulted to fame with the publication of his first novel, *English August: An Indian Story*. A semi-authobiographical novel, it is the tale of an Indian bureaucrat, Agastya Sen. Chatterjee's descriptions are highly evocative and the nostalgia and boredom of Agastya Sen are shared by his creator. The novel is the outcome of an intense, personal experience. Agastya, 'an intellecutual cast among the philistines,' is a misfit in the Indian admistrative set-up. His ennui is due to his failure to come to terms with his environment. He misses his vocation. *The Last Burden*, Chatterjee's second novel, is a domestic novel portraying middle class life in the tradition of Jane Austen. The uncouth and stilted style rob the novel of much of its charm.

Vikram Seth's *The Golden Gate* is a bold experiment in Indian English fiction. It is a novel in verse. The novel deals with homosexuality, an aspect consciously avoided by earlier writers. The structural complexity becomes an artistic imperative for Seth. His second novel, *A Suitable Boy* is a typical Victorian novel. Marriage is the subject of this novel and Seth's treatment of the theme evokes comparison with Narayan. Seth gives a didactic slant to the narrative by making Latha, the protagonist denounce passion. Seth's predilection is for arranged marriages. Liz in *The Golden Gate* rejects passionate love and resolves to marry a friend. Thus renunciation of passion becomes a recurrent motif in Seth's fiction.

The eighties saw the rise of ethnic fiction in India. Rohinton Mistry, Firdaus Kanga and Boman Desai are Parsee novelists who employ English as an instrument of self-discovery. Parsee fiction in English voices the ambivalence, nostalgia and dilemma of the vanishing community. In this fiction, the 'operative sensibility' is Zoroastrian. The Parsee novelists have forged a dialect which has a distinct ethnic character. The tempo of Parsee life is fused into their English expression just as the tempo of Jewish life has gone into the best work of Saul Bellow and Bernard Malamud. The triumph of Parsee novelists in the use of English language is due to westernisation and exposure to the alien culture. Their prose is interpersed with Persian words and Gujarati expressions.

B.K. Karanjia's *More of an Indian* deals with the subject of mixed marriage. The narrative offers a progressive Zoroastrian vision. Farrukh Dhondy's *Bombay Duck* depicts an exile's search for roots. Firdaus Kanga's *Trying to Grow* is an autobiographical novel which derives its strength from the author's trauma. Rohinton Mistry's *Such a Long Journey* offers a vivid glimpse of the disintegration of the Zoroastrian community in the post-Independence era. It also marks the return of Indian English fiction to the traiditional mode of narration. Dina Mehta's *And Some Take a Lover* is the first Gandhian novel written by a Parsee. The narrative highlights Roshni's inner journey from falsehood to the path of *Asha*. Boman Desai's *The Memory of Elephants* is a major work in Parsee fiction in English. Homi's tryst with the collective unconscious transforms the fantastic into the familiar. His fruitful encounter with the racial past shows him a way to control the past, at least in his imagination. The ethno-centricity of Parsee fiction has truly added a new dimension to the canon of Indian English fiction.

The contribution of women novelists has restored balance in Indian fiction in English. Cornelia Sorabji, a Parsee whose father embraced Christianity, could be regarded as the first writer in fiction, though she produced no novels. Her crusading zeal made her a champion of the 'second sex' in India. *India Calling* and *India Recalled* are valuable social documents for they provide us with details of the prevailing socio-economic quandary in which Indian women were haplessly placed.

Among the post-Independence women novelists, Nayantara Sahgal, Kamala Markandaya and Anita Desai are the major figures. Nayantara Sahgal's women characters are blue-blooded. Their material needs are met but their emotional aspirations remain unfulfilled. Ennui pervades their complacent existence. The women in Kamala Markandaya's fiction are victims of poverty, hunger and exploitation. Rukmani in *Nectar in a Sieve* is a symbol of woe. Kamala Markandaya highlights the evil effects of urbanization and modernization on rural India.

Anita Desai deals with the psychological problems of Indian women after marriage. Marriage which results in an identity crisis in an Indian woman's life, becomes the motif of her early novels like *Cry, the Peacock* and *Voices in the City*. Her women characters are rebels, fighting against the two-value system of India which is essentially Manu-made. The commandments of Tennyson too went into oblivion with the arrival of writers like Anita Desai and Shashi Deshpande on the literary scene.

Maya, Manisha and Sita fail in their quest for fulfilment but the magnitude of their effort cannot be ignored.

Shashi Deshpande emerged as a complement to Anita Desai. Her preoccupations are sociological. She questions in her fiction the inferior status granted to women. Her heroines are rebellious and dynamic who refuse to say 'Yes.' In her fiction, the clash is between an imaginative individual and a ruthless society. Shashi Deshpande's fiction is one of protest and her commitment to the cause of women is Woolfean.

II

There are sixteen papers in this anthology. G. Balarama Gupta in his paper entitled "Promoting Indian English Literature: A Plea Renewed" stresses the need for indigenization of Post-Graduate Courses. Indian writing in English is yet to find uniform and unanimous recognition though it is being nourished and sustained by writers like Anand, Narayan, Raja Rao, Ezekiel, Rushdie, Kamala Markandaya and Anita Desai. It is high time people stopped feeling apologetic about this new literature. The paucity of primary and secondary sources is a major constraint for young researchers. Annotated lists of theses and dissertations related to Indian writing in English will be immensely useful. More journals, devoted exclusively to Indian writing in English, are required. He argues that young researchers should be encouraged to explore new areas for their doctoral studies instead of repeating work on Anand, Raja Rao, Narayan, Anita Desai and others. One should cultivate a correct attitude to the subject. A centre exclusively for Indian English literature will be a welcome step.

Prem Nandakumar's paper focusses on family relationships in Indo-Anglian poetry. From the very beginning, she observes, Indians writing in English have commented upon family relationships with high seriousness because the traditional heritage of India gives great importance to the family unit. Despite a certain thematic over-indulgence with love (or lust) outside the knot of matrimony, the family idea is very much with the Indian poets in English. All the major poets including Ezekiel, Ramanujan, Shiv K. Kumar, Parthasarathy and Kamala Das celebrate family life in their works. K.R. Srinivasa Iyengar's *Sitayana* exhaustively presents Sita as a daughter, sister, duaghter-in-law, wife and mother. It is heartening to see the Indian English poet documenting the social truth about the Indian family which may prove to be of great poetic, historical and sociological interest in the twenty-first century.

M. Rajagopalachary and K. Sampath in their paper titled "Fictional Treatment of the Decline and Fall of the Indian Prince: A Note on

Select Novels" seek to examine the fictionalization of the decline and fall of the Indian Prince by Anand, Malgonkar and Markandaya in their respective novels. *The Private Life of an Indian Prince, The Princes* and *The Golden Honeycomb*. These novelists attack the princes for their pomp and pleasure, luxury and sloth, intrigues and feudalistic ideas. They portray vividly the splendour and predicament of the princes who suffered a lot after India's Independence. The decline and fall of the princely system offers a rich potential for the three novelists under study. Anand's faith in democratic socialism is seen in his attack on feudalism and its vices manifest in the princely system. Malgonkar's treatment of princely ways is realistic but biased. Markandaya's portrayal of princely life is more comprehensive than that of Anand and Malgonkar.

Ranga Rao's essay on Narayan entitled "Contemplative Tiger" is a tribute to, and an assessment of Narayan, the writer. Ranga Rao examines the forces that shaped Narayan's vision. His 'complex simplicity' and commitment to work and life are highlighted. Narayan is no recluse; human relationships are sovereign for this gifted writer. He enjoys life and the secret of Narayan is that he is firmly planted in this world. His career was built as much on self-discipline as on self-faith. Ranga Rao's essay provides a glimpse of a few hitherto unexplored dimensions of Narayan's life.

V. Rangan's paper on Narayan's *Talkative Man* studies the theme and the treatment by the novelist. He refers to the various mythical parallels in the narrative. The design of the novel is loose and episodic. The movement is circular with Rann at large again at the end. Rann is a combination of Marco and Raju. The novel derives its strength from Narayan's experiences as a journalist in Mysore. The mood captured in the novel is characteristically Indian. It is not the individual voice of Narayan that tells the story but the voice made polyphonic through a process of dialogism.

P. Hari Padma Rani's paper is on Nirad C. Chaudhuri's *A Passage to England*, a much discussed work. Chaudhuri's accounts are highly evocative. In his hands, comparison becomes doubly functional. On one hand, it helps define England clearly and on the other, it defines India better. Hari Padma argues that many a critic has taken objection to Chaudhuri's remarks. When one faces diametrically opposite cultures, the differences come into a sharper focus. However, certain sweeping statements made by Chaudhuri cannot be swallowed easily. She concludes that Chaudhuri's portrayal of India is realistic, though unpalatable to most nationalist Indians.

T. Asoka Rani's paper entitled "Nayantara Sahgal's *The Day in*

Shadow: A Feminist Perspective" attempts to establish Sahgal as a feminist writer. The heroines of Nayantara Sahgal strive to realise their self-hood either consciously or deliberately. However, Sahgal's brand of feminism does not reach out to the aggressive dimensions of gender-consciousness as reflected in the works of her western counterparts. Nayantara Sahgal portrays Simrit as an embodiment of self-respect and independence. *The Day in Shadow* is a feminist text in which the novelist brings to the forefront Simrit's struggle for liberty, equality, compatibility and self-reliance.

Ravi Nandan Sinha in his paper entitled "Anita Desai's *Cry the Peacock*: The Triumph of the Philosophy of Flux" argues that Anita Desai's fiction attests the validity of the Heracleitian doctrine that all living is essentially flux, and what is generally called 'being' is merely a change from one state of consciousness to another. Maya in *Cry, the Peacock* is an idea as much as a temperament. She is a self divided between the past and the present, between security and fear. Her attempts to reach out to Gautama can be construed as her efforts to come to terms with a truth outside herself. Thus the apparent dichotomy between flux and fixity of life is resolved in *Cry, the Peacock*.

In his paper entitled "Superstition and Psyche in Anita Desai's *Cry the Peacock*," M. Rajeshwar studies the predicament of Maya from a new angle. Superstitious beliefs are attributed by Freud to suppressed hostility. Maya holds Gautama responsible for her unfulfilled instinctuality in the marital relationship. In spite of her sexual frustration, Maya does not cross the bounds of marital morality. In her case, there is a transition from neurosis to psychosis. Her murder of Gautama is not an accident but the result of a prolonged psychic struggle.

Latha Rengachari and E. Manickam in their paper on Indira Ganesan's *The Journey* study the role of memory in the evolution of an individual's conciousness. Memory often filtered, fragmentary, shifting, incomplete and subjective is one determinant of history. All the journeys of the novel form a fine mesh of history—present and past—which throws into relief the journey of Renu into maturity, into an understanding of the present. Renu's journey into the collective memory of the island and her own personal memory serve to put the past in perspective and to redefine her own existence in the present. The novel refuses to be seen as literature of nostalgia or as an ode to a glamourised past tradition, as much Third World Literature is.

Ragini Ramachandra's paper on Vikram Seth records some first impressions on *The Golden Gate*. She observes that the radical departure of Seth from convention is both the strength and the weakness of the novel. She concludes that thematically, the novel has the potentialities of serious fiction, but the extremely quizzical mode of handling of material reduces the book to the category of an entertainer.

E. Satyanarayana's paper studies two short stories of Arun Joshi titled "A Trip for Mr. Lele" and "Survivor." These stories touch on the varied issues that predetermine the existence of man. Mr. Lele's sentimental concern for his deformed child gives the story a huamn touch. In "Survivor," Arun Joshi effectively employs the device of dramatic monologue to reveal the inner self of Kewal Kapoor, the protagonist. Being alive to their inner selves, Mr. Lele and Kewal defy the system which tries to encroach on their personal freedom. A transformation from conformity to confrontation is discernible in both the stories. Arun Joshi seems to suggest that love alone can sustain human relations and impart meaning to existence.

C.N. Srinath's paper on Arun Joshi's *The Apprentice* discusses the relevance of this novel in the present context. The novel has an intrinsic artistic relevance which is not totally dependent on the socio-political scene it portrays. It is neither an existentialist novel nor a confessional story. It is a typical Indian tale which goes to the deeper resources of the tradition to seek more than snap soultions to problems. the detached tone in the novel is reminiscent of Camus's *The Outsider*.

In his paper entitled "The Great Shashi Tharoor Show," Mohan Ramanan examines Shashi Tharoor's second novel *Show Business*. The novel does not offer much; it is built on thin air. Bombay's film world is its focus. Nothing in Bollywood is what it seems. Everything is make believe. Mohan Ramanan concludes that Tharoor's writing is part of a fictional culture in India where clever writing seems to be the order of the day.

Narendra Kumar's paper is on *Trying to Grow* by Firdaus Kanga, a Bombay-born Parsee. He contends that *Trying to Grow* is a *Bildungsroman*. The novel is autobiographical and derives its essence from the strength of the novelist's conviction that it is very rewarding to be considered ordinary. The archetypal conflict in Zoroastrianism is internalized in Brit's passage to adulthood. Written with compelling honesty, this novel offers a rich slice of Parsee life in the post-Independence India.

S. Krishna Sarma in his paper entitled "Indo-Anglian Critical Scene: Notes towards a Perspective" discusses the existing critical scene in India. Parochialism and subjectivity are the major stumbling blocks for a literary critic today. An ideal critic is one who is objective and honest in his assessment, sincere and candid in his approach. Srinivasa Iyengar is a *sahridaya*, a model critic, who attempts to see all sides of a writer and discover the sources of his artistic strength. He is a critic who should be emulated by all aspiring judges in literature.

III

Indian English literature of the post-Independence era exhibits a rich thematic diversity and technical innovativeness. *Midnight's Children, The Golden Gate* and *The Memory of Elephants* are fruitful experiments in imagination. The 'magic realism' of Rushdie, the 'ethnic anxiety' of Boman Desai, the existential predicament of Sealy and the bi-culturalism of Mistry have truly enriched Indian writing in English. This literature is deeply rooted in Indian ethos. Hence its genuineness. Besides familiar voices, one hears new but authentic voices today. The Indian English writer has many miles to go before this literature attains the stature of American literature.

Promoting Indian English Literature: A Plea Renewed

G.S. BALARAMA GUPTA

As the title of my paper indicates, this is a plea I've made more than once. That there should be a need for it even after two decades of this literature acquiring academic respectability is indeed sad, but I believe I can't help it.

One of my strongest convictions is that the syllabus of our P.G. students in English needs to be indigenized. And this involves the introduction of Indian Writing in English, along with Anglo-Indian Literature in English Translation, as a compulsory curricular subject, and not merely as an optional paper. My over-two-decade-long experience of teaching post-graduate students has led me to the painful inference that their linguistic equipment and capacity for literary appreciation have so alarmingly and steadily declined that asking them to study British Literature straightaway would not be a wise strategy. The characters, situations and social mores enshrined in these works are so alien to their experience that they make such a heavy demand on their intelligence and imagination as cannot be easily met by most of them, let alone involve them to the extent needed for a full realization of their value or significance. I, therefore, would suggest we begin with Anglo-Indian Literature, pass on to Indian Writing in English, and then to Indian Literature in English Translation, and only then to British Literature, American Literature, Commonwealth Literature, and so on.

Though Indian Writing in English has been gaining increasing acceptance in Indian universities, it has yet to find uniform and unanimous recognition. Today none but the incurably chauvinistic would shut his eyes to the merits of the considerably substantial body of Indian English Literature which is being nourished and sustained by writers like Anand, Raja Rao, Narayan, Rushdie, Chaudhuri, Anita Desai, Kamala Markandaya, Sahgal, Ezekiel, Dom Moraes and Keki Daruwalla—to mention just a few names—most of whom have won international approbation and recognition. Indian English is hardly any longer a term which calls for ridicule: it is an authentic variety of English, "different from English English. Not *very* different, but different," as Alastair Niven puts it in an interview with Anita Kuryan and Annie Chandy Mathew (*Literature Alive*, Vol. 2, No. 2, September 1988). It is now being increasingly realized that Engliish does not mean British English alone but that it can be Australian English or Caribbean English or African English just as it can be Indian English also. It is high time we stopped feeling apologetic about Indian English and Indian English Literature which, in any case, cannot be wished out of existence. A study of Indian English Literature would give our students an idea of the change that English language has undergone at the hands of Indian writers to suit their culture and experiential needs. In other words, it provides a historical perspective on the nativization of English. It is also likely to inspire our creatively-inclined students to undertake writing in English.

Concomitantly, I am aware that it is the duty of all lovers of Indian Writing in English to realize their responsibility in providing adequate tools for a meaningful study of this literature.

It is unfortuante that even after three decades of the introduction of Indian Writing in English as a curricular subject, our students and researchers are harassed by paucity of both primary and secondary sources. The seriousness of the situation is borne out by some of my own experiences. The other day when I planned to write an article on Bhattacharya, I had to get the necessary material from America. And on another occasion when I needed a photograph of Narayan for a special number of my journal on him, it is again America that I was forced to procure it from. The irony inherent in these situations should wake us up to our responsibilities.

Let me now mention some of our urgent needs. Our first and most pressing requirement is an authentic and up-to-date bibliography of both primary and secondary sources. Then we need an Encyclopedia or at least a Companion to Indian English Literature. We also need the complete works of at least our older and more important writers like Isvaran, Vekataramani, Sarojini Naidu, Toru Dutt, G.K. Chettur, S.K. Chettur, S.V.V., and Harindranath Chattopadhyaya. We further need the Selected Works of modern writers like Ezekiel, Parthasarathy, Jayanta Mahapatra, Keki Daruwalla, Kamala Das, Pritish Nandy and Ramanujan.

Our next need would be a series of critical biographies like the ones which were issued by Arnold-Heinemann and Twayne. Monographs of the kind that have been released by Macmillan on Indian English Kerala writers like A.S.P. Ayyar and Menon should also be welcome.

Annotated lists of theses and dissertations related to Indian English literary themes and writers would be immensely helpful to our research scholars, particularly to avoid duplication.

It is embarrassing to note that we have but one or two journals deovted exclusively to Indian Writing in English. We certainly need more of them, though I am aware of the difficulties involved in managining a literary periodical in our country.

In foreign countries, I learn, there are agencies which specialize in supplying newspaper clippings. Our researchers are sure to benfit from some like them.

Time and again I have been pleading for the establishment of a Centre exclusively for Indian English Literature, a la ASRC for American Literature and Dhvanyaloka for Commonwealth Literature. The need for a Centre like this can hardly be overemphasized. I am of course trying to establish one like this in Gulbarga. I have christened it as NIRIEL—National Institute for Research in Indian English Literature, and this will hopefully gain momentum by and by. Apart from this, I would suggest that each of those English Departments interested in the promotion of Indian English Literature can 'adopt' an author. Mysore University, for instance, can adopt Narayan or Raja Rao and build up a sound library on that particular author and encourage research on him, run a journal devoted to him, and also issue periodical bibliographies and monographs.

Another way of strengthening Indian English literary studies would be to encourage our research scholars to explore new areas for their dissertations instead of repeating work on Anand, Narayan, Raja Rao, Anita Desai, Kamala Markandaya and similar other authors on whom so much work has already been done, unless of course they have something stunningly original to say about them. Indian English non-fictional prose, for instance, is a vast and virgin area which should claim the attention of our M.Phil. and Ph.D. scholars.

Apart from these details what is important for a healthy promotion of Indian Writing in English is the cultivation of a correct attitude to the subject. That lies in a balanced view—neither blind adoration nor fanatic derision. Even as we can be legitimately proud of the excellent creative writing produced by writers like Anand, Narayan, Raja Rao, Desani, Ezekiel, Parthasarathy, Ramanujan, Anita Desai, Kamala Das, and a host of others like them, let us not forget that a lot of trash also is being perpetrated by some others. Our university English departments should produce not only good creative writers but a band of genuine and fearless critics who can sift the grain from the chaff and have the courage to tell poets from poetasters and critics from criticasters. There may be reputations to be pulled down and reputations to be revived.

Family Relationship in Indo-Anglian Poetry

PREMA NANDAKUMAR

Literature is refined social documentation. Shorn of the mid-day glare of facts and figures, chronological surveyings and the bitterness of real life, the essence of our living is made permanent by linking it to imaginative experience. Then is the real Truth made manifest. Ever since man began to go in for literary documentation, social history has not lacked vital inputs. In fact, for almost all the historical details of the ancient past, our most reliable guides have been great poems. The *Iliad* and the *Odyssey*, the *Ramayana* and the *Mahabharata, Chilappadikaram* and *Manimekalai* are priceless treasures that mirror our Greek, Aryan and Dravidian past with great accuracy. They are all intensely human documents that reveal a good deal about familial relationships. The sadly beautiful parting scene between Hector and Andromache, the fraternal love between Rama and his three brothers, the righteous anger of wifely chastity imaged in Kannagi are all familiar instances.

At the same time, there is never a one-side view of the relationships projected by our ancients. We do come across the adulterous relationship between Paris and Helen, the fratricidal war between the Pandavas and the Kauravas, the tragedy of faithless Sali, mother of Aaputhran. Indeed, if we wish to have a total view of familial relationships then and now, we must go to the classics.

The loving togetherness of a husband and wife—total strangers hitherto—is one of the most astonishing wonders of human civilization. And how succinctly it is brought out by Chembulappeyalnirar of the Sangam period:

My mother and yours
Who were they?
My father and yours,
How were they related?
Me and youself,
What paths did we traverse?

Loving hearts here
Have welded together
Like rain water
Fallen on red earth.

It was also realized even then that marital incompatibility was an evil one lived with in society. Hence Avvaiyar's famous advice:

It is wonderful to live together
With an understanding, chaste dame.
But if she cared not for bounds
Better take to asceticism.

Even after the modern age ushered in interviews, court cases and statistics to produce social history, literature remains the best reflector of reality. Among new literatures in India, the youngest is the corpus written in English. From the very beginning Indians writing in English have commented upon family relationships with high seriousness because the traditional heritage of India gives great importance to the family unit. Parents and children, husbands and wives, brothers and sisters, grandparents, uncles, aunts—there is an almost unbelievable nectarean love that flows through these relationships as documented by the first generation Indo-Anglians. One of the earliest poets was Govin Chunder Dutt whose pardonable pride in his gifted daughters and son—Aru, Toru and Abju—has found poetic recordation. Of Abju:

Most loving is my eldest, and I love him most;
  Almost a man in seeming, yet a child. . . .

Aru is "pure and mild, as evening's early star" while Toru is

  Puny and elf-like, with dishevelled tresses,
Self-willed and shy, ne'er heeding that I call,
  Intent to pay her tenderest addresses
To bird and cat,—but most intelligent. . . .

Accurate evaluations too. It is melancholic to realize that all the three died at a very young age. Toru herself was to give us two immortal poems on the heavenly childhood that came to an end too soon because of cruel fate. 'Sita' speaks of the ancient story as retold by Toru's mother in the garden:

But who is this fair lady? Not in vain
She weeps,—for lo! at every tear she sheds
Tears from three pairs of young eyes fall amain,
And bowed in sorrow are the three young heads.
It is an old, old story, and the lay
Which has evoked sad Sita from the past
Is by a mother sung . . . 'Tis hushed at last
And melts the picture from their sight away,
Yet they shall dream of it until the day!
When shall those children by their mother's side
Gather, ah me! as erst at eventide?

The cry of irreparable loss with which the poem closes is echoed in 'Our Casuarina Tree.' The tree reminds Toru of the happier childhood days when she played in its shade with them:

O sweet companions, loved with love intese,
  For your sakes shall the tree be ever dear!
Blent with your images, it shall arise
In memory, till the hot tears blind mine eyes!

The husband-wife relationship was also often a subject for these poets. Govin Chunder Dutt and Manmohan Ghose were loving husbands who blessed their life's companions through poetry. P. Seshadri's sonnet in memory of his dead wife is characteristic of such verse:

Which look of yours is graven on my breast?
  Is it the one, when, with that gentle smile
Of yours, you hail'd me with a kindly zest
  That evening? Or when we drove awhile
Beyond the town, in neighbour forest-shades,
  You wandered at the mightly wrecks of time
Scattered about those hallowed, silent shades?
  When bending on my latest book of rhyme
You wished to know each song? Or, when that night,
  That full orbed moon aglow upon your face,
You gazed with rapture from the terraced height
  Upon the Ganges draped in dazzling rays?
Or when that morn you slowly said 'farewell,'
Struggling with varied thoughts which seemed to swell?

Elsewhere one did hear a jarring note or two. The best known poem on this aspect of marital love is Sarojini Naidu's *The Temple: A Pilgrimage of Love*. A trilogy on the varying stormy phases of husband-wife relationship, it opens with the section 'The Gate of Delight.' A year's separation introduces a chasm in their relationship leading to the wife's agony and hysteria in 'The Menace of Love.' The final section is 'The Sanctuary' when a new life of togetherness begins as total surrender holds the key to understanding and deeper love:

> Strangle my soul and fling it into the fire!
> Why should my true love falter or fear or rebel?
> Love, I am yours to lie in your breast like a flower,
> Or burn like a weed for your sake in the flame of hell.

It is said that the situation presented in *The Temple* sonnets is based on a parallel experience of love, rejection and surrender that Sarojini went through in her married life. The family, of course, meant much to her and such surrender was paid by her willingly as a tribute to her happy motherhood, to her maternal pride recorded in lines weaving the significances of the names of her children, Jayasurya, Padmaja, Ranadheera and Lilamani. Thus Sarojini about Padmaja Naidu:

> Lotus-maiden, you who claim
> All the sweetness of your name,
> Lakshmi, fortune's queen, defend you . . .
> Lotus-maiden, may you be
> Fragrant of all ecstasy.

The problems experienced by Sarojini in her married life were the harbingers of further trouble to the Indian family unit because of the large-scale participation by women in our freedom struggle. Presently freedom came, but no peace for the family. Modern times in the West blew a strong breeze into our traditional patterns upsetting many settled usages. The last fifty years have been a period of impossible strain on our family life, a point excellently documented by the Tamil novelist Sivasankari in her *Palangal*. The joint family system is gone. Western education with its over-doing of the equality image has upset traditional checks and balances like filial obedience and parental responsibility. These changes are sharply etched in the English poetry written by Indians. But though we are willing to rebel, we are not too ready to put the thought into action. Inhibitions are frowned at bravely, but very few of us are ready to cross the magic line of tradition. As a result, an ambivalence has crept in our attitudes.

It is true that an overwhelming amount of English poetry is published in India throughout the year. All the same, very few poets are really concerned with the gigantic problems faced by man living in an increasingly poisoned earth which is poised perilously on the brink of a nuclear disaster. Most of the poets exhibit only conventional jottings of extramarital man-woman relationship. But almost all of them reserve a lyric or two to some aspect of one's familial life as if to prove that they do have some faith in their roots. Often it is in the shape of childhood memories. Again, a few writers do put in a footnote on husband-wife relationship or the miracle of parenthood. What is surprising is that even this tiny fraction (albeit repetitive) turns out to be a fair mass of familial poetry that has undeniable sociological relevance.

Traditionally Indians are committed to respect their parents. The *matru devo bhava* injunction has been deeply imbedded in the Indian psyche as may be noticed in Indo-Anglian poetry. Even a random sampling shows the deep respect and love that the word 'mother' evokes. Such is Hemant Kulkarni's *pitripooja* in *Burning with a Smile*:

> I remember
> mother telling me
> of her delight
> when she was pregnant with me:
> Every evening she lighted a lamp
> on the altar of God
> and prayed for a light inside me
> as I was growing
> into brain and heart
> to be ready for the world.
>
> I have felt that inner light
> all my life
> knowing it to be
> my mother's gift.
> If my body and mind
> dissolve into a shadow
> that light would always abide.

Even in loving homages, other voices do creep in. Dom Moraes's attitude towards his mother is suggestive of the sorrow due to her mental breakdown and the image of his maimed motherland blends with that of his real mother:

Your eyes are like mine.
When I last looked in them
I saw my whole country,
A defeated dream
Hiding itself in prayers,
A population of corpses . . .

Sorrow has stopped your eye.
Your dream is desolate.
It calls me every day
But I will not enter it . . .
Forgive me my trespasses.

A like ironic distancing is Keki Daruwalla's approach:

Your memories flounder
amongst your sons now
you confuse the one who
wet his bed
with the one who
  bit through your dugs
  and made them septic

Parents are ubiquitous presences in the works of poets like A.K. Ramanujan (*Relations: Poems,* 1972), R. Rajeswar Upadhyaya (*Faking Realities*, 1964), Imtiaz Dharker (*Purdah*, 1988) and Hemant Kulkarni (*Burning with a Smile*, 1982). Mostly, the sentiment is predictable. Gratitude for a happier, care-free childhood.

There are startling messages of bitter truth that do strike us now and again. Nar Deo Sharma's "Letter from a Lost Daughter" (*Melody of Wounds*, 1984) is a sheer cry of anguish to turn the focus on struggling parents who try to get their daughters married into a comfortable household:

Until I die my mother will
Remain pregnant with worries.
From the diary of your grief
Papa I dug out the truth that
God drowned in your lonely tears.

I can't forget the agonizing memory
Of your skeletal, blistered struggle

For me in the quest of
A well-paid, educated man who
Rated beyond your poor dreams. . . .

I have removed your bier of worries:
Let me face the hard world alone.

While there are these grating voices, motherhood itself is looked upon with proper pride by Christine Gomez in 'To be a Mother' (*Yatra*, 1989) and Yajna Sri Nambiar offers an Indian girl's defiant reply of love in "An Unseen Poem" (*Yatra*, 1989) to Sylvia Plath's desecratory Occidental filial hate in 'Daddy.' Unlike Sylvia's verbal assassination of the father, Yajna Sri is truly a daughter of India:

I am ineffectual—
To my father.
I am an Arjuna
To my father's Janardhana.
But Krishna was the charioteer
Who with compassion
Proved to Dhananjaya where he failed.
He loved him not the less
For his weakness.

The birth of a son causes termless wonder too. Shiv K. Kumar's cerebral phraseology is not devoid of a certain charm as he welcomes this "third traveller on the road to Emmaus" into his home in *Woodpeckers* (1979). A.V.S. Sarma can produce likeable jingles for his son (Sarma, like Kumar is also a Professor of English) in *Revelations* (1982).

Despite a certain thematic overindulgence with love (or lust) outside the knot of matrimony, the family idea is very much with Indian poets in English. Even when they have alienated themselves from the families either by marriage or exile, an occasional family reunion is welcomed with pleasure albeit couched in ironic phraseology. R. Parthasarathy's 'Homecoming' (*Rough Passage*, 1977) celebrates a reunion (probably during a typical Tirupati wedding) made up of childhood remembrances:

each one pulled,
Sitting cross-legged on the steps
of the choultry, familiar coconuts

out of the fire
of rice-and-pickle afternoons.

When we move to maturer years in one's life, there is a marked difference of tone. The passion of pre-independence days becomes rarer. Marital relationship is watched with ironic eyes and castigated often as a mechanical contraption set up by tradition. Rina Sodhi's 'Indian Women' (*Selected Poems*, 1981) is so typical:

Love
comes like nausea
to an Indian woman
she sighs
she groans
Marriage
is arranged
more sighs
more groans
Motherhood
is unplanned
she spreads
like jungle fire
from the flesh to the bones
Life
is a matter
of 591 milestones
285 sighs
286 groans.

Nissim Ezekiel, however, finds wedded love passion enough in 'Marriage Poem' (*Collected Poems*, 1989):

Between the acts of wedded love
A quieter passion flows,
Which keeps the nuptial pattern firm
As passion comes and goes,
And in the soil of wedded love
Rears a white rose.

Some poets give importance to intellectual companionship which is much stronger than mere platonic love. Rabindranath Menon's 'Letter from a Divorcee' (*Pebbles on the Shore*, 1981) dissects the several steps of marital incompatibility:

> Marriage couldn't be a
> union of hearts alone for those
> with heads. Intellect must be equally close.

But when there is a union of hearts, nothing can really come in between, asserts Ashok Mahajan in 'Partners' (*Vivisections*, 1980):

> The bride
> Possessed no trousseau
> Save her tresses.
> Her groom's wages were
> A wad of words.
> Yet they showered
> Their meagre gifts
> Upon each other
> Like confetti. . . .
>
> Such monsoon-fling of youth
> Left them legacies.
> Aging together, they watch
> Both fungus and the algae grow
> As lichens upon their hyetal tree
> In rich symbiosis now.

In any case, more often than not, even if beaten, the Indian wife (mostly the rural variety, though) would rather stand by her husband against interfering (even if well-meaning) strangers, ruefully exclaims Polanki Ramamoorthy in *Rangoli* (1985):

> who the hell are you?
> How dare you raise your hand on my man?
> He is my husband—
> why shouldn't he beat me—
> but who the blasted hell are you?

It is hard to come by a poetess dissecting her husband but Kamala Das rises to the challenge in 'The Stone Age' which is actually an embarrassing ode to adultery:

> Fond husband, ancient settler in the mind,

Old fat spider, weaving webs of bewilderment,
Be kind. You turn me into a bird of stone, a granite
Dove, you build round me a shabby drawing room,
And stroke my pitted face absent-mindedly while
You read. With loud talk you bruise my pre-morning sleep,
You stick a finger into my dreaming eye.

Quite a few men pay extravagant tributes to their life's partners. In fact Adiyar's *Wife* (1987) is a sumptuous exercise that rings paens to her who is a willing slave.

But my wife . . .
Has shackled me with the Thali
Aroung my legs
Keeps me on the pedestal
Of her sanctuary.

It is rather strange that brothers and sisters are not considered in Indo-Anglian poetry these days. Probably the nuclear family has made this a distant past now. One vainly searches for a poem like Toru's *Sita* in these volumes. An occasional exception certainly brightens our day. Eugene d'Vaz's 'Two Little Brothers' (*The Fire Rose*, 1981) exquisitely recaptures the early dawn of brotherly togetherness which vanishes in the harsh midday sun of middle age. It is a paradisal image which can be seen only in one's memory:

I was once like you.
Now my intentions are muddled.
The world threw faggots and boulders
On our way
Till our days got fouled
Till the wind stopped singing and howled.
He goes his way, I mine.
And 'Brother' is just another
Of those stupid words.

Once we enter this territory of family relationships in Indo-Anglian poetry, a staggering amount of material gets piled up beggging us for statistical analysis and critical commentry on the emerging trends. For, it is not only parents, husbands, wives, and children who people this world. There are also cousins and aunts, uncles and in-laws. And grandparents. Grandparents viewed as curmudgeonish crones by poets like Ashok Mahajan or remembered with understanding pity as in Jayanta Mahapatra's well-known poem 'Grandfather' (*Life Signs*, 1983) on Chintamani Mahapatra who embraced Christianity during the terrible Orissa famine of 1866 since he was starving and on the point of death:

> We wish we knew what it was to be, against dying,
> to know the dignity
>
> that had to be earned dangerously,
> your last chance that was blindly terrifying, so unfair.
> We wish we had not to wake up with our smiles
> in the middle of some social order.

God's plenty here. And if we added up K.R. Srinivasa Iyengar's epic, *Sitayana* (1987) to the corpus, we have a whole view of ideal family life. For *Sitayana* exhaustively presents Sita as a daughter, sister, daughter-in-law, wife and mother. In spite of all the sorrows and exile, there is no sense of alienation in Iyengar's Sita for she is capable of being very much an individual and at the same time ably interweaves herself as part of the larger web of life.

> She was conscious all her yesteryears found
> their meaning in the present.
> Which in its turn forged its seminal links
> with all that's yet to be born.
>
> Here on the left, the past, and its tally
> of fulfilments and failures:
> and here on the right, the unborn future:
> the present justifies all.
>
> And so Maithili, tired but contented,
> rested in peace for awhile,
> and now refreshed and happy, was ready
> for the tasks of motherhood.

It is heartening that the Indo-Anglian poet doesn't shy away from experimenting with any compound in human experience and is right now documenting the social truth about the Indian family which may prove to be of great poetic, historical and sociological interest in the 21st century.

Fictional Treatment of the Decline and Fall of the Indian Prince: A Note on Select Novels

M. RAJAGOPALACHARY and K. SAMPATH

The paper seeks to examine the fictionalisation of the decline and fall of the Indian prince by Anand, Malgonkar and Markandaya in their respective novels *The Private Life of an Indian Prince, The Prince*s and *The Golden Honeycomb*. The princes have been attacked by those novelists for their pomp and pleasure, luxury and sloth, intrigues and tiger hunts and their feudalistic ideas. These writers have dextereously delineated the splendour and predicament of the princes who suffered their political and material ruin after India's Independence.

Statistics reveals that once there were as many as 565 Maharajahs reigning over 12.8 lakh sq. kms. of Indian territory and 75 million subjects. From the biggest kingdom of Hyderabad which stretched over 2.11 lakh sq. kms. with an annual income of Rs. 8.5 crore in the 1930s to the smallest 800 bigha Katodia state in Gujarat, their opulence symbolised the Raj grandeur. This grandeur was lost after the Independence of India. Though some kings like those of Mysore got annual privy purse of 26 lakh and continued to live in richness, for most the pension was just enough to make both ends meet. For example the king of Katodia got just Rs. 192 a year. With the abolition of privy purses by the then Prime Minister Mrs. Indira Gandhi in 1971, the deathknell was rung for the princely system. Some ex-Rajas like Scindia, Karan Singh, Mansur Ali Khan Pataudi earned a niche under the new dispensation. But some became deranged and decrepit paupers unable to reconcile to their changed lots. Their existence became chaotic with property disputes and dire straits.

The decline and fall of the princely system forms a mementous part of the Indian history and it has offered a rich potential for fictional presentation by Anand, Malgonkar and Markandaya. These three novelists have written a novel each on the life of an Indian prince. Anand's prince in *Private Life of an Indian Prince* is a lunatic; Malgonkar's prince in *The Princes* is an egoist who prefers death to surrender, while Kamala Markandaya's prince in *The Golden Honeycomb* is a rebel. The latter seems to be far in advance of his counterparts. The princes have been attacked for their weaknesses.

II

Of all the novels of Anand, *The Private Life of Indian Prince* has a historical theme and offers interesting insights into the world of princes in India. It reveals the author's own mental agony after an immense personal crisis and nervous breakdown. Anand wrote it in the "white heat" to "purge his system" for the hill-woman whom he loved, who not only made him divorce his wife but ultimately discarded him in favour of a better catch. The hill-woman served him as a model for Ganga Dasi, whereas Anand nozzles "his own emtional breakdown" through prince Ashok Kumar. Anand explains:

> My knowledge of Indian life at various levels had always convinced me that I should try to do a *comedie humaine*. In this the poor, the lowly and the untouchables were only one kind of outcastes. The middle sections and the nabobs and rajas were also to be included as a species of untouchables. Unfortunately, there has not been time to show the poor-rich of our country, who deserve pity more than contempt.[1]

Anand successfully interweaves the material for his purpose in order to make it interesting to the reader. He brings out the peculiarities and fancies of the prince in detail. Through the first person narrative, Anand projects the historical facts effectively. The narrator in the novel is Dr. Hari Shankar. And in the "Author's Note" to the novel, Anand cautions us: "The natural 'I' of the first person singular has tended, in this book, to become a character in his own right. The 'I' in the novel is not to be mistaken for the author."[2] Though on several occasions the narrator speaks for the author, Anand is right in insisting that he should not be confused with Dr. Hari Shankar, as Dr. Shankar is more often than not the disembodied voice of reason and sanity. He is actually modelled on Lala Man Mohan, a liberal gentleman who was private secretary to the Late Maharaja of Patiala. This dissociation of himself from the narrator helped Anand caricature some aspects of his own emotional life in the persona of Maharaja Ashok Kumar. There is as much of Anand in his prince as in the narrator, and this partly accounts for the penetrating analysis of the Prince's character. Dr. Shankar is the rational side of the author analysing the irrational side as seen in the prince. Dr. Shankar knows the king's mental predicament and the private lives of the princes. Dr. Shankar is the spokesman of democratic humanistic socialism. He finds feudal monarchy an anachronism and champions the cause of the proletariat, but at the same time he just cannot abandon the joys of the court's luxury. Feudalism is the main target of Anand's criticism in *The Private Life of an Indian Prince*. The ideals of liberty and democratic socialism are upheld, and the evil of cruelty is reproved.

Anand views this novel as a historical document in the ways of Indian prince. The interest of the novel lies in the effective portrayal of the decline and fall of the Indian prince through the protagonist Maharaja Ashok Kumar, popularly known as Victory or Vicky. He is described as the fast fading species of Rajas, raos, Nawabs and princelings whose "knell was so conscientiously and effectively tolled,"[3] by the first Home Minister of free India, Sardar Vallabh Bhai Patel in 1947. The resentment of Indian princes can be understood, if the historical data is examined from time to time. In 1858, Queen Victoria and King George V asserted and reaffirmed the protection of all the Princely states of India. On February 1921, the Duke of Connaught read the royal proclamation in response to the princes's demands headed by Sir Ganga Singh, the Bikaner state ruler, assuring the privileges, rights and dignities of the princes of India.

On July 5, 1948, Sardar Patel issued a powerful appeal to the princes that invited their patriotism and disarmed their apprehensions. He asked them to sign the Instrument of Accession. This act compelled the princes to accept; some of the princes died, some became mad and some princes "wept like a child" and some rulers got heart-attack after signing the Act. The Nizam nawab and Bikaner ruler even disobeyed the Instrument of Accession at first. After India's Independence, the decline of the princes came gradually with the 26th Amendment of the Indian Government in December 1971 abolishing the privy purses of the princes concerned. Anand portrays the predicament of Prince Victor against this backdrop in his *The Private Life of an Indian Prince*.

The Private Life of Indian Prince starts with a public scandal, Maharaja Ashok Kumar's rape incident with Bunti Russell. The prince is saved by A.D.C. captain Pratap Singh. Ironically he "found no evidence of rape, but there has been an attempt of penetration." (37) And when he wants to see the prince, regal rage is at its pitch. Dr. Shankar, the keen-witted and sceptical narrator, accepts the prince's plan to lodge a complaint with the Deputy Commissioner against Captain Russell for the comments against the sacred person like Maharaja Ashok Kumar. When the Deputy Commissioner rejects it, the prince feels like a rat in a hole and wants to do something very drastic to mend the situation in to which he had got himself.

The Bunti-Vicky episode shows Anand's delineation of princely order and their feudal, aristocratic inherited royalness with minute eye. Maharaja Ashok Kumar is a clever, spoilt womaniser on the brink of political and personal disaster. He participates in broad gestures, melodramatic speeches, and strange histrionics to avert the inevitable disaster. Dr. Hari Shankar, the narrator, knows that the agony of the prince is not physical but psychological.

> For his intelligence seemed to have run riot through the large gaps in his educaation and experience. And this made him pick up many things, with which he was trying to form a single thing but which made him a bundle of ill-assorted fantasies and facts, whose incongruous collection into one personality made him a strange, wild creature. And yet he was not so ill-assorted as his mistress Ganga Dasi, because he was comparatively constant while she was absolute promiscuity. So it was touching to see the clashes between the poetry and prose of his life, the contradictions that arose from his reflection of the feudal, aristocratic idea that all excellence is inheritance, and the sense of direction which dictates integration through the discovery of values in the new society. The spirits of his dead ancestors were pulling him towards the old virtues, prowess, splendour, firmness, dexterity, generosity, heroism in battle and the other duties of the high-caste, superior, Kshatriya prince, while a number of new demons, the fashions of the hour, were pulling him into another direction, on account of the shameless schooling through which his childhood in his father's zenana, and his boyhood and youth in the hands of the Angrezi Sarkar, had put him. For he had learnt alll the filth that his retinue of servants in the palace could teach him, and been spoiled by his doting mother, always anxious to save his life against the homicidal fury of his father's concubines. (42)

Vicky's lustful devotion to his seductive and tigerish 'femme fatale' seems to be motivated by his Oedipus complex. Even though his mother-fixation in his childhood cannot make him 'surrender to any woman completely,' (10) he attached himself later with charming, megalomaniac Gangi. In spite of the fact that he feels no security in Gangi, he feels in her general amiability and charm, consolation such as he cannot get from the company of "his chaste, rather proper wife." (82) And while he suffers the agonies of hell owing to Ganga Dasi's incalculable temperamental fits, he is fascinated by the challenge of her moods, by the "excitement and thrills of those changing colours, of which her vanities, frailties, fickleness and cruelties were the secondary hues as against the lush splendour of the primary colours of her lusts and passions." (82-83) She inflames, delights, controls and ultimatcly destroys him. Vicky has become mad and neurotic due to Gangi's "absolute promiscuity." The prince loses Gangi who runs away with his political secretary and the Indian Government forces him to sign the Instrument of Accession.

On the political plane Vicky has to tackle attacks from guerillas and his cousins, Sardars and the praja mandal. Besides these, the states Department forces him to sign the Accession Act. Vicky meets the challenge with his foolish boasting and self-deluding lies and he talks about his genius which nobody understands and compares himself with Sri Ram Chandra. He goes to Delhi to meet Sardar Vallabh Bhai Patel where he is asked to wait indefinitely hurting his pride. At last the interview is granted at five o'clock in the morning and Sardar Vallabh Bhai Patel makes him sign the Act. Exiled in London due to his madness he seduces a shop girl with "Princely finesse." But, he cannot forget his mistress and has her paramour murdered only to end up in a mad house from the shock of what he had done. The act of murder recoils on him and precipitates his final insanity. Maharaja Ashok Kumar, in a lunatic asylum, craving for Gangi becomes despaired as his wife Maharani Indira attends on him tenaciously with all the tenderness of a woman whose love for her man was "selfless and real." Vicky's gestures and utterances in his mad mind touch on the major chords of his previous days. They reflect the past glory. In his madness he expresses the factual truth of the past fancies.

Anand's *The Private Life of an Indian Prince* is thus a powerful indictment of the weakness of Indian kings and princes. Anand takes a sociological perspective in portraying the decline and fall of the Indian Prince. His faith in democratic socialism is seen in his attack on feudalism and its vices manifest in his princely system.

III

Malgonkar has transmuted history into fiction in his *The Princes, A Bend in the Ganges, The Devil's Wind* and *Cactus Country*. Of all the novels of Malgonkar *The Princes* is regarded as the best for its portrayal of the recent past viz. the decline and fall of 565 princely states and what Lukacs calls the "present as history." Malgonkar wants to unfold "the thoughts and ideas of a somewhat tightly-knit social groups,"[4] viz. the

Indian princes. His association with the princes has provided an insight into the human and cultural values embodied in their strange lives and his training as a historian helped him to understand, with detachment and objectivity, the anachronistic irrelevance of princely India as a socio-political phenomenon and the evils associated with it. He has chosen "an ordinary educated man" to be the last prince of an imaginary state Begwad which is already in the process of disintegration.

The historical material supplies the spine of *The Princes*' narrative and the centre of its interest. In the backdrop of the novel are the events that took place in India between 1938 and 1958, the years just before and after Independence. The historical record is clear enough. At the time of partition in 1947, the future of 565 princely states remained unresolved. The Indian Government, the Menon-Patel-Mountbatten team succeeded in integrating 565 princely states by signing the Instrument of Accession Act in August 1947, which marked the end of British Raj as well as of Indian princes and the beginning of free India and Pakistan. *The Princes* is the fictional treatment of the plight of the princes who disappeared from history. E.M. Forster who recorded his experiences in an Indian state in *The Hill of Devi* finds 'numerous and heart-rending' parallels between his experience and that portrayed in *The Princes*.[5]

Malgonkar's familiarity with the princely life is clear from his statements and two of his books of "straight" history dealing with the life and times of the princes, viz. *Puars of Dewas Senior* and *Chatrapathic* of Kolhapur. He said in an interview:

> My grandfather was the prime minister in one of the bigger states in India and I grew up . . . knowing the princely ways, knowing their peculiarities, knowing the little things that they did different from other people, knowing their little vanities. But that contact grew when I started my profession as a big-game hunter—anyway, I was for a little while a professional big-game hunter and my clients were the most monied one could think of, were American millionaires or Indian princes and one of them invited me to write history of his family. So that gave me long enough contact, close contact with his family and with their attitudes and with their peculiarities to be able to write a book about princes.[6]

Malgonkar has camouflaged the Maharaja and his son of Puars of Dewas Senior with his creative imagination. He has reshaped the facts into fiction. This reshaping can be ascertained with some examples. Malgonkar changed his highness Sir Tukoji Rao III, K.C.S. I, Maharaja of Dewas state Senior into his Highness Sir Hiroji, the fourth K.C.S. I

Maharaj of Begwad, and his son Maharaja Vikramsinha Rao, later called Chhatrapati Shahaji, into Abhayraj Bedar III. Malgonkar recreates a historical situation, places his "composite" characters in it and portrays how they would act in such a situation. In this process, the historical character Hiroji and Abhayraj appear to be fictional characters. Malgonkar delineates the situation without any tampering. The dates, the historical facts, the conferences between the princes and the Viceroy, the privy purses etc., are carefully presented. The nationalist movement of India is mirrored in a masterly fashion. Malgonkar does not compromise with historical facts. The novel is not a mere historical record from within but a human exploration of the passions of an extinguishing race.

Prince Abhayraj, unlike his father, favours the freedom movement and Gandhian philosophy in *The Princes*. The Maharaja hates the nationalists because he never accedes to sign the Instrument of Accession, instead he courts death in an open war with fierce Kolar tigers. And, he never wants to lose his kingdom. The Maharaja believes: "There will always be a Begwad, and there will always be a Bedar ruling it—so long as the sun and the moon go round." (11) The British Rajas were in chaos, as the British paramountcy was to lapse on 15 August 1947. The princely states had to face the sorrowful event of their fall. The prince says: "I was aware that I was in the presence of sorrow; a grief deeper than when his brother had died, a humiliation far more wounding than when his Maharani had taken a lover." (265) The Maharaja's heroic qualities were unshaken even after his administrative powers came to an end. The King reinstates his own flag, even when the Praja Mandal hoisted their flag at the Administrative building.

The Princes is about Abhay's evolution through the conflicting forces of loyalties and ideologies. He sees the emergence of the third force to safeguard his Begwad. He says: "But I would prefer the British to the Gandhiites any day, so that the integrity of our state is preserved for all times. It is more important than anything else—*more important than our lives,—yours and mine.*" (16, italics mine) The father is tyrannical, arrogant and reactionary but the son is a bit more realistic. But, at last the son also yearns to satisfy his father's instincts. He confesses later that though he differed from his father initially, he has gradually come to identify himself with his ideology. "I myself went a long way towards sharing his [father's] views and values as far as our state was concerned. Indeed it seems to me that with the passing of the years, *I have come to identify myself more and more with these values, with the result that today I feel myself a spokesman for whatever the princely order once stood for.*" (18, italics mine) The crux of the novel is the complex relationship between father and son. Clashing at first, they grow closer as the book draws to an end with the princly states fighting for their very existence against India. Abhayraj becomes the ruler of Begwad for exactly forty-nine days.[7] The young prince realizes that the princely states will collapse. "To a keen observer like Abhay the princes were like ripe mangoes in late May. All ready to fall and some were downright rotten. All it needed was for some one to come and give the tree a shaking. They would all drop off good and rotten alike." (267) The process of Abhay's identification with the old order becomes complete with his flogging of Kanakchand, the Dalit Education Minister, in public. "I saw him close, staring at me in utter disbelief, insolent no longer but cowering, shrinking frightened; the face of a schoolboy in the grip of terror. I raised the crop high. I brought it down 'This I have sworn,' I was muttering to myself '*This I have fulfilled.*'" (342-43, Italics mine) The whipping scene at the close of the novel should be viewed as a serious blemish as it demands suspension of disbelief to an incredible extent with its strange suggestion that a fallen prince could flog a Minister and yet go scot free for the simple reason that the latter happens to be a Harijan.[8] It shows the writer's partiality towards the royalty.

The novel also reflects the princely attitude to love. The Maharaja would allow Minnie to be his son's mistress but not wife; for Abhay, Minnie is an object of lust and not of love. He had illicit love with Zarina the concubine pampered for him. Love affair for the prince is a taboo. The prince marries Kamala, the eldest daughter of the Raja Akheti, with his father's approval. But it was "a marriage of convenience" and a social obligation to make a Maharani for the kingdom. The Maharaja has also ill-treated his wife as an untouchable. She was discarded and "left like a leper." She had to suppress her desire "to live the life of a normal woman." (163) The Prince pities her and advises "to break away before it is too late." (163) But when she elopes with Abdulla Jan to Karachi, he fails to appreciate her act like his father.

Thus Manohar Malgonkar presents the princely ways, their vanities and peculiarities realistically in *The Princes* without, of course, taking sides.

IV

Of all Markandaya's novels, *The Golden Honeycomb* (1977) alone deals with the historical theme. It portrays the decline and fall of an Indian prince. In this stupendous novel, we come across a series of touching events, pitiable strikes, baffling agitations and lockouts. The novelist turns her attention to the freedom struggle. In the prologue, Markandaya presents the country as a dominion in British possession. The commercial minded East India Company had the subtle intriguing nature to hold on to India and conquer its princely states one by one. It becomes all the more incumbent upon Britishers to hold on after the Declaration of Independence by the USA in 1976. The popular statesman Lord Randolph Churchill, delivering his speech to M.P.s appealed to them "to watch the most sedulous attention, to develop with most anxious care, to guard with the most united and undying resolution, the land and the people of Hindustan, that most truly bright and precious gem in the Crown of the Queen, the possession of which, more than that of all your colonial dominions, has raised in power, in resource, in wealth and authority this small island home of ours . . . has placed it on an equality with, perhaps even in a position of superiority over, every other Empire of ancient or modern times." This declaration foretells the British view in India to adopt all kinds of tactics to bring the princely states under their rule. Markandaya, dexterously mixing 'fact with fiction,' presents the emasculation and alienation of royalty from their people through an ingenious British scheme, the subsidiary Alliance, which reduced the princely states to mere "golden honeycombs."[9] This novel reveals the best imaginative effort of Markandaya's consciousness and her most ambitious, brilliant workmanship of art.

The novel gives a vivid description of the luxurious and voluptuous life of the Indian Princes, the durbars, decorations and other paraphernalia of the royalty. A.N. Dwivedi says: "This novel is not only her best imaginative effort to project the development of national consciousness but also her most ambitious and brilliant work of art. It reveals at once her extraordinary sense of conscious realism and historicity, unmatched in Indo-English fiction and only rarely evident in contemporary British fiction."[9] We find a thematic shift from the typical East-West encounter to Indian freedom struggle in her later novels. The story treated in the novel concerns the Devapur State whose ruler, Bawajiraj I, is deposed for his so-called seditious activities. The agent, an Englishman, and the Dewan, a shrewd Brahmin serving the state as Chief Minister, exercise their minds to choose as their ruler a Kshatriya youngman of eighteen years who is recently married to a girl of thirteen. He ascends the 'Gaddi' of Devapur as Bawajiraj II. The British had picked him up for a Raja because they wanted him to be a puppet in their hands, not independent in anyway. He lives in pleasure with pomp and show of being elevated from a mere landowner's son to being Maharaja. But Bawajiraj II meets with an accident in a hunting spree and dies prematurely, leaving behind his wife and son. The son succeeds to the throne as Bawajiraj III, is the benign Maharaja of a rich and prosperous Indian State.

Bawajiraj III performs his duties conscientiously. He enjoys his leisure. He hunts, he rides, he excels at polo and cricket. This bland and delightful pattern is interrupted when he falls passionately in love with a dazzlingly beautiful but tempestuous commoner Mohini. The child of this turbulent union is Rabi. Father a prince, mother a commoner, throne dangled in front of him not as a right by succession but as a prize to be conferred by the paramount British power in return for good behaviour, Rabi becomes the focus of opposing influences. Rabi is caught up in the conflict of powerful opposing influences involved in selecting his succession to the Gaddi of his father. The central characters, around whom the story revolves are: Bawajiraj III and his son Rabindranath.

The heir-prince, Rabi is enlightened on several aspects and a nationalist feeling is infused into him by the Pandit, the tutor. This enlightened Rabi's endowments and love of freedom. He hates his father due to his submissiveness to the British Empire. At the instance of his father, Rabi sits on the throne half-heartedly, which shows his disagreement with his father's attitude.

Rabi's capricious reactions at the Durbar have been 'painful realities.' He realises that his father need not be subservient to the foreigners. His love for freedom and keen perception enables him to have knowledge of the inevitability of the people's support for India's liberation. His meetings are successful and the popularity grows and 'the crush gates of the father courtyard' are kept closed. He has become a leader of the people.

Rabi's national awareness is explicit in his conversation with the Maharajah.

> "Your Highness," he said then, "We feel—"
> "'We,'" cried the outraged Maharajah,
> "Who is 'we?'"
> "We, the people," said Rabi, without display, but very plainly. "We feel that insupportable levies and treaties must be rescinded, whatever the consequneces. We shall continue the struggle to that end."
> "In the process you will tear the State apart," said the furious Maharajah.
> "Not I. We," said Rabi, who was equally furious. (46)

He suppresses his father and openly opposes the ways of his father in particular and the monarchy in general. He wants the liberated free India. Maharajah is grieved at the freedom struggle. He consults his son. India achieves Independence and the princes of India are left with two choices. They had to sign the Instrument of Accession and acceding either to India or to Pakistan. By participating in the National freedom movement, he wins popularity and helps to bridge the gulf between the ruler and the ruled.

Kamala Markandaya's portrayal of the princely life appears to be more comprehensive than that of Anand and Malgonkar. S.P. Appa Samy aptly remarks: "Kamala Markandaya's presentation of the life of the rulers of the princely states rings more true than that of either Mulk Raj Anand's version, which is highly coloured for the foreign market, or even Manohar Malgonkar's, which does show some decay rather than development and change. She is at great pains to present the growing national feeling and the insidious way in which national feeling invades both private and public life." Markandaya's presentation appears to be as authentic as that of Malgonkar, though it has a deeper psychological probe into the historical characters.

NOTES

1. Shyam M. Asnani, "The Indian Princes: Their Portrayal in the Indo-English Novel," *Commonwealth Quarterly*, p. 85.
2. Saroj Cowasjee, Introduction, *The Private Life of an Indian Prince* (New Delhi: Orient Paperbacks, 1972).
3. R.K. Kaushik, "Indian Princes Again," *Literary Half-Yearly* (Mysore), Jan. 1971.
4. Author's Note, *The Princes*, p. 7.
5. Letter to Malgonkar, dated August 27, 1963
6. James Y. Dayananda, *Manohar Malgonkar's "The Princes": History in Fiction and Fiction in History* (Boston: Twayne, 1974), p. 95.
7. It is quite interesting to note that Malgonkar wrote this novel exactly in 49 days. He says "I wrote it in 49 days and bring those 49 days into the book. I make my maharajah go through 49 days, just to sort of pinpoint the number."
8. Kamala Markandaya, *The Golden Honeycomb* (London: Chatto and Windus, 1970), p. ix.
9. A.N. Dwivedi, "*The Golden Honeycomb*: A Critical Appraisal," *Perspectives on Kamala Markandaya*, ed. Madusudhan Prasad (Ghaziabad: Vimal, 1984), p. 208.

Contemplative Tiger: R.K. Narayan at Home and Abroad

RANGA RAO

Q: What would you rather be in your next birth?
A: 'A contemplative tiger.'

Interview in *Sunday*, Calcutta, January 1988

'I just want to be left alone!' said Narayan to an interviewer sometime after the publication of his memoir, *My Days* (Chatto, 1973). That plea carried with it, I suspect, an uncharacteristic desperation, coming '*after* an hour's fruitful conversation'; it was also a sentiment of success: and now you had his own memoir, precluding the need for more probes. But the magnitude of Narayan's success makes inevitable a comparable interest in the man; the contemplative comedy of Narayan's novels is the expression of a rare personality. Who is the real Malgudi man?

Narayan is extraordinary for modern times: even to those who do not associate writers and writing with abnormal psychology. A man cannot be creative (so we have come to assume) who is robustly sane. We remember the boastfulness of Hemingway (among Narayan's contemporaries in the west), and, more, his casual cruelty to the mating turtles, turning them up to die in the merciless sun; or we cherish fondly tales of Faulkner's drinking bouts. Narayan has been placed in the same category of creative achievement as Hemingway or Faulkner, as Narayan mentions, with due modesty, in his *Dateless Diary* (Penguin). While John Updike refers to him as 'the foremost Indian writer of fiction in English,' Graham Greene goes further: 'Since the death of Evelyn Waugh, Narayan is the novelist I most admire in the English language.' But the Narayan paradox is impressive; neither the man nor his work is patently 'modern'—far from it, far from any quirks or deviant behaviour, far from any personal philosophy of nihilism or any ism, the Indian writer represents a sanity, a wholesomeness, a psychological fullness which is as stable as humanity. It is the complex simplicity of a rare man, a gifted writer who is at once committed to his work and life, to the living and the dead.

Narayan is in love with this world, a lively Hindu (no shocking contradiction), a South Indian at that, welcoming, for example, 'a god-given opportunity' for a poetic piece on coffee, coffee-making as an esoteric rosicrucian rite, in his American travel diary.

The paean to coffee should alert us to a significant aspect of Narayan: he need not, for a 'modern' writer, grope for his roots, rue his alienation. Narayan is firmly rooted. Responding to an American he meets in the USA, he remarks: "She says that she likes South India more than the North, a very pleasing thing to hear, as pleasing as it'll be for a North Indian to be told that Madras is detestable in every way." Presently, Narayan narrows the focus when another American remarks that he prefers Mysore to Bangalore: 'Excellent sentiment, sir,' says Narayan: Mysore is where Narayan's home is. And, finally, more specifically still, Narayan has his immediate family. 'Roots' mean more than one's home-town and family: 'I'm more than ever convinced that the South Indian diet marks the peak in the evoloution of culinary art. . . . We come to know more of his belonging later: he looks forward to meeting with Professor M.N. Srinivas, the renowned sociologist, an old friend from India: South India-Mysore: because Narayan 'longed to speak Tamil to someone.' Tamil is Narayan's mother-tongue. But Narayan hates cultural humbug. An American refuses to shake hands with him, preferring instead to perform a namaste, the Indian salute. Narayan comments: 'Where is the point in mimicking a piece of Oriental courtesy when you perpetrate occidental bad manners by ignoring a proffered hand?' And, it follows, he has no false patriotism: at a concert by Ravi Shankar, the sitar maestro, in a US city, Narayan observes shrewdly: 'The atmosphere of India is further authenticated by a large cockroach which peeps from under the platform.'

R.K. Narayan is a people man. This writer is no recluse: he is certain to be at home anywhere in the human world—even in the Arctic, all that he will ask for is Eskimos, people, children in particular. This aspect of his personality, too, comes through vividly in his *Dateless Diary*. At Madison, he is entirely at home with the American family, because it is a 'happy household': a happy American home is no different from a happy home anywhere. On the train, westward bound in the States, he enjoys his journey thoroughly because it is people again that matter.

Friendships are quickly established. Again and again, throughout the tour of an alien land, the warmth touches us: he can surprize us by mentioning 'A deep friendliness abiding for three hours': a contradiction in terms for lesser humanity. Human relationships are sovereign for

Narayan, even fleeting ones: 'Human beings knit up in all fantastic unbelievable ways, complex and unexpected links.' Though rooted in his place and milieu, this novelist is capable of wide kinship. And when he departs, he is seen off 'by the entire family who manage this motel.'

Simplicity is integral to Narayan, representative of the predominantly rural ethos of India. He hates travel and is convinced that he is unfitted to even packing for it (but is today the jet-set writer of India); and loves, as any self-respecting Indian would, the casualness of the railway service in Santa Fe. Without a wristwatch, he is perhaps unique as a traveller to the States who can talk of a 'timeless existence in the heart of New York.' Yet, for a vegetarian and teetotaller who hates all contraptions, he manages without much ado his long tour of the USA—the land of 'comfort, gadgets, and beef-steak.' And promptly, child-like, he is hooked on American TV.

He can be boyish: a friend does not take him along to a meeting 'for fear that I might behave frivolously or utter loud, cynical remarks at the meeting.' This self-knowledge is not too dependable however: he claims he is 'too experienced in film world'; yet not long after he is taken for a ride by the filmwallas in India and also by an American friend in the staging of *The Guide*. He is one of us in human vulnerability, seriously upset when a drop of blood appears at his nostrils: 'It completely spoilt the day for me. Could hardly manage to write fifty words for the day; became a prey to all morbid thoughts.

More happily, Narayan's mind can be agitated by other thoughts. He turns down the offer of an apartment because of the address: 'Haste and Telegraph': he might have 'nightmares of "Haste makes waste" or people might address my letters: "Post and Telegraph." The mere name of a person can set this adult innocence off on a pure comic gambol: he cannot talk to a woman because her name is Mrs Keyhole: 'I could not concentrate on business as my inner being clamoured to know if "KEYHOLE" was being mis-spelt.'

The same man can seriously talk of 'need for prayer and meditation in daily life,' yet he declares: 'Religion is not a thing that anyone can openly avow—it's like one's underwear.' For this Indian writer a conversation has to be ended when it becomes 'too long,' he prefers wandering in the garden.

The secret of Narayan is that he is firmly planted in this world, often showing pure enjoyment in just 'looking around.' He diverts himself at the August U.N. playing with pushbuttons, pressing the button for a new tongue 'half-way through each sentence.' It is a delight in existence. For a man of such vitality, food is important: 'the first step in self-realization is good food.' The same sensibility can reach out in other directions, too. He can notice that 'women of tremendous beauty' pass by in the crowds; or 'I just continued to sit and look at a pretty girl.' When a secretary commends her own coffee to him because she makes her blend and kisses every grain, Narayan responds: 'I think I'll try it even without cream, you seem to have given it the right treatment.' Naturally, the famous Forest Lawns cemetery is for him a place 'where one might live rather than be dead in.' Earthly beauty fascinates him, at any level: the Grand Canyon is the acme of worldly experience: Here all religions meet and merge, the almighty takes his name here.

The American travel diary confirms for us what we have been told all along by numerous interviewers over the last four decades. Ved Mehta, profiling Narayan in *The New Yorker*, presents an unpretentious, convivial, natural Narayan, with 'a constant expression of innocence.' Narayan is naturally at ease, 'smiling with his eyes and teeth'; but when Narayan talks of his wife's death, 'tears came into his eyes.' Narayan also confirms his partiality for human company: 'Novels may bore me, but never people.' He makes a remarkable professional discovery: 'I find I write best when I have no burden on my mind, when I am absolutely at peace with myself.' Temperamentally incapable of literary anguish, Narayan offers an alternative to *angst* literature. Few modern writers can claim: "If I had to live again, I would want nothing different. I live from moment to moment. . . . Nothing really has gone wrong with me. I am deeply interested in life as a writer. That is perhaps why I have not gone mad." (*The Hindustan Times*, 1973) The exclusive temperament results in a surprising level of social participation. Reviewing Narayan's memoir *My Days* in *The New Yorker*, John Updike calls him 'writer as citizen.' Our writer-citizen is today a nominated member of the Indian Parliament.

Narayan's presence can mislead us; it makes light of a tremendous struggle. Narayan's life is the archetypal story of the self-launched artist: he tells it in *My Days* with characteristic detachment. Typical of the enormous load of scepticism he had to work under was his own father's response to his first cheque as a writer: 'Your first and last cheque, I suppose!' though the old man apologized immediately. The trials and humiliations have not lost their sharp edge, even in Narayan's cool recall of success. Updike surprizes us in an otherwise perceptive essay when he calls Narayan's life 'rather uneventful.' For the real appeal of *My Days*, Narayan's memoir, lies not in its story of success, but in the story of the novelist's early struggle.

When he dropped for good the idea of a conventional job, Narayan recalls, 'They seemed to suspect my sanity' and 'they' well might: it was nothing short of madness to have thought of making a livelihood of writing, and in English, in India—and in the early thirties—before R.K. Narayan. 'In those days, no one could own up to writing stories in India. It was the most penniless thing one could do!' Narayan tells Ved Mehta.

After the death of his father, every adult male in this middle-class South Indian home had to contribute his share to the material needs of the family. And so, from the beginning. Narayan wrote with a single purpose: 'All this amount of composition was to allow me to earn money and help the family,' implying a touching faith in literature as a living, a wildly exotic idea in those days for a non-metropolitan youth.

It was a trying and often desperate situation; but all that Narayan allows himself to say in retrospect is: 'Money was a big worry.' *Self-respect* ruled out short-cuts: 'One shouldn't fall at another's feet.' Narayan hated seeking patronage: 'I hated the very idea.' The struggle was sustained by Narayan over several years: 'thousands of rejection slips,' he mentions to Mehta, giving us some idea of the prolonged struggle.

Narayan's career, challenged by *crippling* circumstance from the beginning, has been built as much on self-discipline as on self-faith. 'I reqularly wrote a few pages each day,' from the very beginning, a rare Shavian commitment. He mentions his 'fear of missing my daily schedule,' of a 'daily discipline,' even touchingly, of 'this weekly grind.' Narayan's journalistic stint too is important: 'a thousand-word literary clowning week after week.' One of the earliest assignments Narayan accepted and executed with professional zeal, was the review of a book, of all things, on Maritime Laws.

The economic struggle—where a half-rupee counted—which Narayan conducted with his aptitude for simple living, strengtened him. Narayan learned to be 'ruthlessly professional': when his essay for *The Atlantic* exceeded the original limit by 250 words, Narayan demanded and received $ 250 more (at a dollar a word). Narayan's early fight for a living has also established a native, middle-class habit of cost-effectiveness. The novelist's frugal habits are shared by his characters. The granny in *Waiting for the Mahatma* is even epigrammatical: 'there is nothing so fleeting as untethered cash.' When Jagan in *Vendor of Sweets* renounces home and son, he goes away *with* his cheque book.

Early experience has also taught him a certain firmness in dealing with people. I myself witnessed this delightful side of Naryan when I interviewed him in 1968. Narayan drew my attention to a discussion on the BBC in which, among the three participants, two, both Indians, a novelist and a poet, ran down Narayan and the Englishman had his hands full defending him. Narayan resented, particularly, the observations and adverse comments of the Indian poet in English: and he added, with a sharpness of which I had not thought him capable, that he didn't care what a 'tenth-rate poet' said about him. Later, on Narayan's next visit to Delhi not long after, I took the transcript of the interview to him and read it out. When I came to the 'tenth-rate poet,' Narayan asked me to hold on, paused for just a second or two, and said: 'Promote him to third-rate.'

'To be a good writer anywhere, you must have roots, both in religion and in family. . . . I have these things,' said Narayan to Ved Mehta in New York. But Narayan carries his Hinduism lightly.

Watching Naryan's quiet Hindu practice, in life as well as in his fiction, we realize that religion to Narayan is like a skin. One is born with it and lives with it. He shuns ostentation in any form. All through *Dateless Diary* we have evidence of a quiet, gentle Hindu identity. However, of the two, family and religion, it is to Narayan's credit that the family takes precedence.

Happy family relationships were the basis of Narayan's childhood. Kunjappa ('little fellow'), the sensitive, timid boy, could not have been more fortunate.

A valuable education the future novelist received from his grandmother included the sagas of South Indian classical music. To this day, Karnatic music is Narayan's chief form of entertainment. He has his own library of tapes and himself plays the veena with impressive skill. He has not missed a single music festival at Madras Music Academy during the last four decades. Behind the novelist's art we can discern the discipline, if not the technical approach, of classical music.

Narayan's sensibility has been further shaped by two later periods. First, by the year he spent among books and writing, following his failure to enter the university. Secondly, the period following his wife's death. For a temperament of Narayan's intenseness, the loss was traumatic: 'I lost my anchorage.' He tells Ved Mehta that he considered following his wife into the funeral pyre, but there was his child Hema, the very likeness of his wife. And Narayan was helped by the same resilience that he gives to his heroes. A new psychic sensitivity which he acquired helped him even to sense the presence of a ghost. He can now talk confidently of 'from life to death and beyond.'

When Narayan built his house in Mysore, he designed his own study to have eight windows to match his own inclusive vision, the wide human horizon, of life and death and beyond.

R.K. Narayan's *Talkative Man*: A Polymythic Palaver

V. RANGAN

R.K. Narayan's *Talkative Man* (1986), claimed to be a short story by the blurb, but described by Narayan himself as a long short story of 116 type-written pages, is the story of an amateur journalist, proud of calling himself Talkative Man[1] (TM) who narrates the story of a futurologist, Dr. Rangan, Rann with a double 'nn' who proves to be an expert not so much in futurology as in the fraudulent art of Casanovism, sowing wild oats around. The staple of the story as related by TM is the attempts of Rann to seduce gullible young women, while all the time professing to be working on a UN project on a cannibal weed, known as Congress weed, the parthenium, which is supposed to destroy all life in the world. Rann, at the beginning of the novel has just come from Timbuctoo to Malgudi whose peaceful atmosphere would facilitate his writing his project report quietly. Of course, it remains unwritten till the end of the book. He has time only for philandering. He keeps on gazing at the ceiling, perhaps, to plan heart-conquests; as the weed on which he is working is going to conquer the planet, earth, Rann destroys women's hearts. In both, the generating principle is the victim. Rann's search for future life on earth ends ironically in his running for his life, but it does not prevent him from leaving behind him a long trail of broken hearts and bastards.

TM who opens and ends the story compares himself with Narada, the legendary broadcaster of gossip, perhaps the first journalist or media man to have carried news across the continent without satellites or other technological props or electronic gadgets. Narada is also the originator of many *Puranas*.[2] TM is the Narada of the *Bhavishyatpurana* of which Rann is the protagonist. The story of a futurological expert turns out to be a modern tale of Don Juan. As the time scheme in any *purana* is puzzling, in this *Rannayana* too, the time of action of Rann's sex-fights and the resultant flights—an inverted epic or mock epic—strains the reader's credibility a little: a post-modernist fluid fictional time scheme. At the time of Sarasa's marriage with Rann, she has just completed 18 years in May 1978. She is separated from Rann for twenty years, which means that when Rann turns up at Malgudi, he is around 40 years old, because in 1978 he is supposed to be studying in Madras Loyola College. The year of his appearance at Malgudi is 1998. The novel is dated 1986. Is it about future then, and consequentially about a futurologist? But the narration is in the past tense. The post-script is in the present tense. Time Past and Time Present are fused with Time Future so as to make the action timeless, because there is no dearth of debauchees in the ancient as well as modern age. As long as there are gullible girls, there would be no scarcity for lechers, disguised as prophets, experts, scholars etc.

Narada is a *Kalahapriya*, a lover of intrigues, and his intrigues always do good to the virtuous and bring about the punishment for the wicked, an instrument of ancient poetic justice: TM's efforts to reunite Sarasa and Rann are well-intentioned. Like Narada who sometimes would speak half-truths, if not total lies, to mislead people with a view to doing good to them, TM also is evasive in his replies to Sarasa's enquiries about Rann. Even the harm that he is supposed to have done to the wicked and the wayward ends in their good. Upto a point, TM tries to protect Rann, but once he realizes the dangerous game Rann is playing with Girija, TM thinks it imprudent to remain a silent spectator, and steps in to stop the calamity. This is a typical Narada-like timely intervention. TM also practises, like Narada, dissimulation by feigning ignorance so that those whom he has to protect are not exposed to danger. Narada is generally a catalyst in the actions initiated by him. Here TM is also uninolved in the drama of Sarasaá-Rann-Girija tangle. But from another angle, TM may be viewed as the omniscient narrator who can destroy his characters as the fictional requirement demands. He is at once the saviour and destroyer of Rann. He saves him first from the Station Master and then from Sarasa. He destroys Rann by abetting Sarasa in getting him kidnapped—a comic irony! By a double reversal, Rann, accused as a young man of having abducted Roja (Sarasa then called), is now kidnapped. The former kidnapper turns into the present kidnapped, and the then kidnapped, now kidnapper. How neatly the tables have been turned, a typical Syngean comic situation! Rann is paid back in his own coin—the engineer hoist with his own petard, a sort of poetic justice meted out by TM-Narada narrator. After the Lotus Club fiasco when Malgudi people discuss Rann as a potential terrorist, TM keeps quiet: "I never corrected any statement nor defended Rann. Not my business."[3] This is from the man who said earlier: "I decided to save him from wifely intrusions." (63) Is TM then the anti-self, the articulate self of the normally reticent Narayan? Are all novelists Ancient Mariners who only wait for an audience, and in that way they are all talkative men? Sometimes the talkative men are overwhelmed by more vociferous persons. Imagine one of the characters talking more than the author. As in Pirandello's *Six Characters in Search of an Author*, Narayan's characters seem to be waiting in the queue to be transported into the novels (vide his own statement in the post-script, crisply illustrated by R.K. Lakshman in the book). Sarasa finds the author of her story, TM, and reduces him to a silent listener by her chatter. She is a character in TM's story. TM time and again says that it is only a story. The characters in the illustration are waiting for Narayan to open the fictional door; thus there is a coalescence of reality and illusion, truth and appearance, and the novel becomes an interesting study of errors—a comedy of mirrors!

If TM is Narada, we have to think of other characters in terms of *purana personae*, and try to find some correspondence between the fictional men and women and their mythological counterparts. The most obvious myth that is hinted at by Verma at the end of the novel is Savitri going in search of Satyavan's life and redeeming it from Yama. Here Rann is the composite of Satyavan and Yama-husband and lady-killer. The novel then burlesques the original myth. There is no direct encounter between Yama and Savitri *nee* Rann and Sarasa here as in the myth. But the early part of her life runs parallel to Savitri's. Savitri chooses Satyavan, despite Aswapathy's not objection but fear of Satyavan's impending premature death. Like Savitri's, Sarasa's marital life is also short-lived. Satyavan is claimed by Yama, the god of death, and Rann by parthenium, the weed of death. However much Rann was caught in the weed project before the advent of Sarasa in Malgudi, after her arrival, he has done very little in that direction, which means that not by direct encounter but through proxy, TM, Sarasa is waging a war against the death-dealing project to redeem Rann-Satyavan. She redeems him by a ruse as Savitri outwits Yama through his own boon. Rann-Yama is tricked into a car, and Rann-Satyavan is claimed back by Sarasa-Savitri. What happens later, Rann running away with Komal, a nurse in St. Matilda's, becomes irrelevant to Malgudi, the *locus* of the *purana*, because it happens at Delhi, and hence beyond the purview of TM-Narada. Or would Satyavan, matched with an aged wife and bored of life with a super woman have started in quest of pastures new, if the original myth had been extended? This story being a parody may admit of such a comic possibility.

TM-Narada may be involved in another myth, the *Mahishasuramardana* (The Taming of the Bull). When TM starts narrating the story of Rann, he sits under the Mahishasura calendar in the Boardless, and first describes the *asura* elaborately. Bull is traditionally a symbol of sexual virility. In Tamilnadu, there is a practice to dedicate a bull to a temple and leave him free into the town or village. This bull is so sacred that nobody should do any harm to him. He may enter the market place and eat anything out of any shop, and he should not be beaten at all, because he is a *kovilmadu*, the temple bull. A fellow who goes about sowing wild oats is very often described as the temple bull which has a right to mate with any cow. Rann is the bull (*Mahisa*) let loose on the world, philandering and impregnating women right and left. Like an *asura*, who can assume different forms (*kamarupa*), Rann travels with several aliases in different places with different passports, a globe-trotter like an *asura*. Every *asura* has his own sweet time, and then comes the moment of his destruction. Sarasa, the pistol-wielding motherly figure (Home-guard), standing for all women duped by Rann-Mahisa, in her Home-guard uniform looking formidable and forbidding (reminiscent of Kali's battle array) is engaged in the war against the evil *asura*. The *asura*, a *mayavi*, eludes her grasp, but every *asura* has an Achilles' heel, and who should know it best but Narada; here TM leaves detailed instructions to Sarasa about how to destory Rann by kidnapping him. One *asura* may be destroyed, but a hundred may crop up. Only then, there would be a justification for *avatars*. Rann-Mahishasura may be tamed or killed, but only for a short while. His latent *asuric* nature, a genetic possibility hinted at by TM at the beginning of the story, surfaces and he runs away with Komal, the nurse. This time what *avatar* would Sarasa take? She might say, vide the Post-script, that he would destroy himself by his own duplicity; not an external enemy, but an internal would kill him, because evil is self-consuming and self-destructive.

TM may be taken as that garrulous old man, the tireless eavesdropper and meddler, Polonius in the *Hamlet* myth; all authors are veritable eavesdroppers or voyeurs! Three or four references in the novel to *Hamlet* suggest this view. Rann, as a young student of Loyola College is a scholar and gentleman, like Hamlet in Germany. Rann loves Sarasa sincerely and arranges for their marriage, as Hamlet's love for Ophelia is genuine and he entertains the idea of making her his wife. On her father's advice, Sarasa betrays Rann, accusing him of having kidnapped her and then confirms it in the court, as Ophelia betrays Hamlet's trust in her by spying on him at her father's instigation. Sarasa's father who speaks very little is the *dopplegonger*, the double of TM. Polonius is proud of having exposed Hamlet through his daughter. It is only after the betrayal that Rann's attitude to women changes and it looks as though he thought of the 'frailty' of women and decided to exploit it. He takes it out on womankind, which explains his ditching many a woman across the continents. Gertrude and Ophelia have undermined Hamlet's faith in women; Sarasa's mother and Saarasa have eroded Rann's trust in women. On Sarasa's own testimony, Rann had not been philandering before their marriage. So his flirtations all over the world are his weapon of avenging his betrayal. His letters and diaries are score books recording the number of hearts he has broken and the number of bastards he has fathered. His *modus operandi* is to strike the woman at her vulnerable points, heart and virginity and leave her bereft of both.

TM becomes a father-figure to Girija and Sarasa in that he is their protector: to Sarasa he restores the marital status and with Girija he averts it. If Sarasa's father had intervened in Rann-Sarasa affair in 1978, TM, who tells Gaffur that Girija is like a daughter to him interferes in 1998, the elopement could not be averted, but in 1998, it is prevented. Caught unawares, Rann-Hamlet has only to lie low and when the time is ripe, he launches his revenge again. Hence his running away with Komal. Rann's first appearance in his three-piece suit, almost ghost-like *cape-ape*, is feared and wondered at by the sentinel, the Station Master, who like the guards, has to keep watch for Seven Up and Seven Down, and performs his regular duties, like Bernardo and Marcellus. Like Hamlet bundled out of Denmark by Claudius through Rosencrantz and Guilderstern, two men decoy Rann into a car to be kidnapped. Hamlet who should have been put to death by the king of England, escapes providentially and comes back to Denmark to complete his task of revenge. Rann who should have been tamed by Sarasa runs away with Komal to continue his drama of revenge. Sarasa's letter indicates that he may be going strong in his lady-killing in the continents. The world is a weeded garden for Rann and like the weed (on which he is preparing a report) feeding on weedicide and growing wilder, domesticity, respect and love of life, its attendant virtues, instead of killing his lechery, feed him to plan his next flight, and the weed has started spreading: his name Rann, with an extended 'n' may suggest this. Sarasa says: "He was an expert really in the art of deception with unsuspected depths of duplicity," (142) an opinion that would have been definitely expressed by Claudius about Hamlet.

In another sense, Rann may be seen as Hamlet. Rann, like Hamlet, is grave, moody, constantly brooding and seldom flippant and is almost always humourless and characterised by an antique disposition which makes him an object of wonder to the Malgudians. His three-piece suit is only a sartorial manifestation of his gravity, because it is a very formal dress. In that way, he may not be a fake specialist or madman as TM would make him out to be. TM speaks almost always in a flippant tone about Rann's research and ridicules his project. But one can notice a certain note of solemnity in Rann's speech at the Lotus Club. Looked at closely, the lecture does not appear to be the vain and shallow call of a charlatan, but a serious warning of a scientist genuinely concerned about the future of humanity and about all life in the world. There is an undercurrent of agony, and the anguished cry comes through in one or two places, in the lecture. TM himself says that Rann has a systematic way of going about his work, the way in which he has arranged his papers and filed the clippings from the old newspapers. Further, TM also states that Rann has been engaged in the 'Journals Room' of the Lawley Library, making copious notes from the back numbers of journals. Rann says that an old Australian planter's journal has given him some useful information.

TM is a journalist interested only in sensationalism, and not an author who shows a real insight into human psychology. His first understanding of Rann, Sarasa and Girija is invariably wrong, and he comes to know well about Rann, Gaffur about Girija. As Polonius claims to have a good sense of judgement and misleads Claudius about the real intentions of Hamlet, TM thinks that he has understood people well, but misjudges them. All his tongue-in-the-cheek description of Sarasa as a forbidding-looking woman in Home-guards uniform is subverted by his own confession on two occasions how Sarasa is essentially a normal woman in her responses and reactions. In that way, TM-Polonius misleads the readers who, like Claudius, would like to know the real Rann, and not the Rann that TM makes him out to be. Perhaps, if Polonius were to narrate the Hamlet story, he would do as TM does Rann's. For all his age and worldly wisdom, Polonius has a strong streak of frivolity about him that makes him a ridiculous old man. Throughout the novel, TM's tone is light and his encounters with Rann and Sarasa smack of banter. He belongs to the vanishing tribe of the landed gentry of Kabir Street whose only avocation is to celebrate festivals, suggesting the mood of gaiety and flippancy, on an elaborate scale and sit on the pyol and gossip away their time. A happy-go-lucky lot, they do not make an effort to understand anything or anybody quite seriously, and they are interested only in what is grist to their gossip mill. A member of such a class cannot be expected to know Rann, a person dedicated to intellectual pursuits. TM can only be loquacious, as is evidenced from his *palaver* pouring forth 'words, words, words.' But he can never fathom the mind of a thoughful man like Rann, just as the garrulous Polonius has not measured the mind of melancholy Hamlet.

That Rann is quite serious about his work is testified by TM's own evidence of having found among Rann's paper a Thanksgiving letter to King Gustov of Sweden for the Nobel prize he might be awarded for his earth-shattering discovery. A person loaded with a suitcase of papers and books cannot be a *poseur*. TM shows very little patience or inclination to understand Rann's work. Hamlet, being the product of the Renaissance, is concerned about moral and religious issues, and Rann, the product of the modern amoral world, shows ecological preoccupation, because the modern world, with all its industrial and technological boom, its 'industrial immorality,' has become a dangerous place to live in, what with its polluted environment threatening to annihilate all life. If Hamlet fears spiritual and moral fall out by the conduct of people like Claudius, Gertrude, Polonius and Ophelia, in the unweeded garden of his world, Rann is worried about the very survival of life as a result of ecological disruption in the weeded garden of the modern times.

Whether Savitri myth is parodied or Mahishasura legend modernized or Hamlet story travestied, none of these is sustained throughout the novel; except in a very general way, the smaller details bear no relation to any one myth or legend entirely. There is a certain patchiness about it. Is it because of its having been serialized? It appeared in a serialized form in *Front Line*, published from Madras. Or has Narayan found his material intractable or is he unable to weld the pieces together and organize them into a neat remythicisation as he has done with Bhasmasura myth in *The Man Eater of Malgudi*? The post-script, instead of helping us, hampers our understanding, when on second thoughts, Narayan adds what TM would have advised Sarasa to do after Rann has run away with Komal, and what her response would have been. This shows that Narayan does not want to end the exploits of Rann, but keep them open.

Even Malgudi which is the District Headquarters in this novel, shows a lopsided growth. It has grown with its new extensions and colonies necessitating the shifting of the cremation ground to a far end. But the Railway Station receives only two trains: Seven Up and Seven Down. There are only two auto-rickshaws and only one taxi, that of Gaffur! All this in 1998! Narayan who is noted for his realism and minute observation of places and people, like Dickens, seems to have lost grip over his material even in this area.

As though to add to the puzzle, rather the muddle, Narayan hints at another folk myth, the wolf and the Babes. He describes Rann as the wolf of the fairy tales. True, Rann seems to specialise in devouring young girls in his philandering game. Though the ages of his victims are not given, it can be assumed that they are extremely gullible sex-wise. Wolf is insatiate in his hunger; Rann's sex-hunger is as insatiate as a wolf's appetite for food. Starting at about 20, Rann has been active even after 40, and threatens to be more menacing even in his old age. As irony would have it, Sarasa becomes the futurologist when she sounds the warning that with Rann-wolf prowling around, no girl could be safe in the future.

Talkative Man, because it is about a talkative man, is a novel of loose design, episodic and rambling. There is no story-line in the conventional Narayan way, and the movement is circular with Rann at large again at the end. TM/author is the omniscient narrator who seems to interfere with the action very often. Rann and Sarasa are static characters, rather flat, the former always a cheat and the latter, ever gullible, reminiscent of Jonsonian characters, and the novel resembles the Comedy of Humours. Despite her fierce facade and domineering tone which is impulsiveness rather than imperiousness, a mere verbal swagger, Sarasa is malleable, Rann is always cool, calculating, watching his steps and waiting for the right moment to strike.

Rann is a combination of Marco and Raju, an explorer like the former and a saviour like the latter. While Marco in *The Guide* is preoccupied with the past life as an archaeologist, Rann is probing the future life. While Marco neglects his wife, engaged as he is in his discoveries, Rann leaves his, and many other women, in his search for the parthenium weed all over the world. Raju's saviourship in *The Guide* is imposed on him by the Malgudians who involve him in a fatal demonstration of his powers; Rann's self-styled saviourship is heckled at the turns almost fatal to him. Both are scape-goat figures: Raju to save the Malgudi people from the drought disaster becomes a rallying point of their hopes. But Rann's self-imposed protectorship is denounced by the Malgudians, because he has become by his discovery, an embodiment of the weed disaster as is seen in the hysterical cries of the old woman in the Lotus Club meeting, supported by the violent vocal protests of the audience. While Raju symbolises hope, and hence to be sacrificed, Rann is a symbol of fear, and therefore to be got rid of. He is also Ramani of *The Dark Room* in his utter callousness towards women who are just sex-dolls for both Rann and Ramani to play with. Rann is Vasu of *The Man Eater of Malgudi* in his *asuric* nature in that Vasu is Bhasmasura in destroying himself ultimately, and Rann is a Kamasura whose *Kamarupa* (assuming different names) and *Kamacharya* (lasciviousness) are, according to Sarasa, going to be his own doom finally.

The pistol-wielding Hedda Gabler-like Sarasa is perhaps intended to be Nora Helmer in *The Doll's House*, the New woman, (*pudumai penn* of Subramania Bharati) but she is that only in a very limited sense. Sarasa enters the traditionally male profession and rises to higher positions.

No doubt, she is not like Savitri in *The Dark Room* to be meekly resigned to her lot by her husband's betrayal. There is an explosion of personality in Sarasa in that she shows a courage and determination to beat Rann down to a discipline, and assert her individuality. But the final picture of Sarasa, for all her bravado, is that of a normal woman who is afraid of sleeping in the open at the Railway Station, though armed with a pistol. More than this, her breaking down at the end when she tells TM about how she should have listened to her father's advice in 1978, scrapes off her veneer of fierceness and independence and reveals her in her true colours as an ordinary Indian woman. She is like Daisy in *The Painter of Signs* in her spirit of independence, but it is a moot point if she has Daisy's will. As though as an after-thought, Narayan infuses into her a strong will in the imaginary conversation between her and TM in the post-script. But the novel proper ends in her The Dark-Room-Savitri-like meekness, the only difference being that Savitri docilely returns to Ramani, while Sarasa cannot even get at Rann. For all her assertion of independence, she is unlike Bharati of *Waiting for the Mahatma* who can twist her lover on her fingers and cause him anxious moments. Bharati's nationalist uniform and Satyagraha weapon are more potent than Sarasa's Home-guards dress and pistol. Bharati gains a soul force from her Gandhism which can annoy Sriram as much as the British. But Sarasa has not imbibed even physical courage from her Homeguardism, because she is afraid of physical assault if she sleeps in the open.

Talkative Man has been drawn from his own experiences as a news reporter soon after his graduation when he did a stint of jounalistic writing in *The Hindu* of Madras. The last minute rushing of the news through the Railway Mail by TM was Narayan's own habit of rushing his weekly instalments to the Sunday issue of *The Hindu* every Wednesday in 1935. As a reporter for *The Justice*, Narayan went round Mysore city picking up odd bits of information at the courts, Muncipal Office, Government Departments etc. Like the TM's flowery and eloquent write-ups being mutilated and condensed by the Editor at Madras, Narayan's reports were also subjected to diminution and disfigurement.[4] But TM is rather puzzling as a narrator in the novel. From the ring-side watching the characters interacting with one another, he moves into the arena to resolve a crisis. He is rather the umpire than a player, so much so that he interferes only when the play becomes rather rough. He acts as a *deus ex machina* rather than a regular actor.

TM's story is narrated by Narayan, and TM narrates Rann-Sarasa story. Narayan, TM and his story have a trinity like quality. Narayan creates the story, but TM sustains and destroys it. The post-script is supposed to hew the rough edges, but it leaves them more jagged. In *puranas* the author is one, the narrator is *another Suta*. Here in this novel also, we have this diarchy. As the Suta's narration is scrappy and episodic, TM's story is also loose and rambling. In the *purana*, we have no access to the author's thoughts with regard to the material and the characters, and here too, we have no idea about what Narayan thinks of TM's story. The post-script with the characters queuing up at his door makes confusion worse confounded. The casualness of TM giving the same number to two trains, Seven Up and Seven Down, there cannot be a greater confusion for the Railway authorities and also saying that Sarasa's father returned from Avadi to Egmore in train, the former being on the Broad Guage and the latter on the Metre Guage section, have the quality of Suta's indifference to time and place in a *puranic* story. That TM's story of Rann unfolds itself from his sporadic narration to Varma at The Boardless is significant in that Narayan having released from the Creator's mind (*Brahmamanasaputra*) has left him free to manipulate his way through the fictional world, watching him bumbling, fumbling and tumbling, like an indulgent parent. Narayan says in his *My Days* that his grandson wrote a short story called "Grand" which was juvenile in its inconsistencies and incongruities. The grandfather liked it for 'the ease with which it conveys in one sweep the complexities, muddles and demands of kinship, and the ups and downs of man's fortunes,'—enough substance to fill a novel.[5] Here is Narayan permitting himself a little indulgence by a Pirandelloesque paradox, by jumbling up the characters and narrators. The incongruities and inconsistencies have a *Puranic* flavour.

Talkative Man has for its subject the fatal weed which was some years ago the sensational news. Topical subjects tend to be reduced to mere gossip, like the day's news being anatomised in a casual manner even today by a group of idle rich people in some families of the leisured class in Tamilnadu. It is a daily sight in some small towns in Tamilnadu to see a group of men sitting either on some house pyol or in a public place like a tea shop or a coffee club analysing national and international news of the day good-humouredly with a great deal of guffaws. One could see them handling dexterously several disparate subjects, like an Indian juggler handling the balls or daggers thrown up at the same time in a continuous course of casualness. *Talkative Man* captures that mood and character.

Mikhail Bakhtin, the Russian Formalist, says that the reader enters a world of polyphony. A polyphonic novel for him is essentially dialogic. The novelist's voice encapsulates other myriad voices, speaks out to the Talkative Man and becomes the written voice we read. Narayan's narrative then combines all the other voices and stories that engender his story and engages TM and the reader dialogically in the story. It is not the individual voice of Narayan that tells the story, but the voice made polyphonic through a process of dialogism. Significantly, the narrator is called Talkative Man: he talks: talks to the reader, weaving the story and as he goes on weaving the yarn, he adds or subtracts, because it is an oral narrative.

NOTES

1. Talkative man, the narrator of many a short story of Narayan, makes his appearance here again as a narrator.
2. Nagaraj in Narayan's novel *The World of Nagaraj* contemplates to write a book on Narada, which shows Narayan's fascination for that *puranic* character.
3. R.K. Narayan, *Talkative Man* (Mysore: Indian Thought Publications, 1986), p. 137.
4. This tongue-in-cheek style tale of Rann's project has its prototype in Narayan's flippant review of Paul Brunton's Egyptian Studies in *The Hindu* of those times.
5. *My Days* (Mysore: Indian Thought Publications, 1974), p. 185.

The Image of India as Portrayed in Nirad C. Chaudhuri's *A Passage to England*

P. HARI PADMA RANI

Given the title *A Passage to England,* one might wonder what one could find of India in a book like this. But the title seems to take after E.M. Forster's *A Passaage to India*, which was published in 1924. A major difference between the two books is that the former is written by a Britisher while the latter is by an Indian. Besides the titles, there are not many significant points of comparison between the two texts. While *A Passage to India* is a purely fictional work, *A Passage to England* is an account of Chaudhuri's visit to England. Being a travelogue, it does not call for much literary discussion.

The immediate question that pops in one's mind here is "If the book is an account of Chaudhuri's visit to England, where could India possibly figure in?"

One must not forget the fact that it is an Indian who is making a passage to England. Having made a passage from India to England, Chaudhuri could not but make use of the tool of extensive comparison in his account of the English life. In the hands of Chaudhuri, comparison becomes doubly functional. On the one hand, it helps define England clearly and on the other, it defines India better. Both England and India are pitted against each other. Therefore the readers will find India "walking in freely" in Chaudhuri's account of England, which makes it extremely interesting as well as enlightening. As Chaudhuri remarks:

> In this account of England, India will be found to be walking in freely. I could not define my sensations about the new country without placing them against those about the only country known to me. One-half of my perception of England was the perception of something not India.

Time and again in the course of the book Chaudhuri keeps comparing the conditions in India and those in England. This gives a piquancy and edge to his writing. Very interestingly, the book begins with a remark on Indian philosophy.

There is virtually no aspect of English life which Chaudhuri does not contrast with that of Indian life. Even the colours of flowers in England are different from those of the Indian ones:

> In England, I found that colour in my country and colour there were quite different things. In our country we have many flowers with blazing colours, but these hues always seem to flow and run into surrounding atmosphere, as dyes which are not fast do in water. In England, on the other hand, I saw floral colours almost as frozen masses. (Part I Chapter II)

Chaudhuri finds the rivers of England more interesting than those of India. He justifies his preference by saying that the rivers of England have a 'scenic complement' which none of the rivers in India has.

In England one cannot make out the social class or status to which a person belongs by merely looking at him or her whereas in India,

> Wherever we go, we notice two kinds of people, the ordinary folks who dress in their own way, speak their own dialects, behave in their own way, without sophistication and affectation, as against the minority who wear the older Hindu or Muslim aristocratic costumes, speak both English and the standard forms of the Indian languages and have what in the west would be called a middle class pattern of behaviour. (Part II Chapter I)

For Indians, noise is an essential condition of cheerfulness while the English people have silent habits. Life in London, even in the most crowded streets, seems like a film of 'pre-talkie days.' After living in the bazaars of India for years, when Chaudhuri sees a sight like this, he feels like crying out, 'the eternal silence of these infinite crowds frightens me!'

Chaudhuri rightly observes that there are no better places than buses and trains to observe the public behaviour of a nation. In India, the buses are full of conversation not only between acquaintances but also between people who have never met before. Nobody minds being used as a cushion. So far as newspaper reading is concerned, the fellow passengers never snatch away anybody's paper, but they take the pages he is not reading, in the most polite manner, and distribute them among themselves. The passengers help one another in many ways. The buses in India are in short a microcosm of Indian life.

In England, people do not disclose their position in the world. If they are authors, they do not refer to their books; if they are statesmen, they do not disclose programmes for reforming the world, whereas in our society a man is always what his designation makes him. Whenever we introduce a person, we always emphasize the official position the person holds. We also see people adding it themselves when the introducer omits to announce their designation.

Evidently Chaudhuri does not say all this in criticism of his people. He is only describing what usually happens. In India obsession with one's designation and degrees is a commonplace phenomenon. Even in a thing like a wedding card, one would not like to see one's name without his or her degree beside it.

Many a critic has accused Chaudhuri of being an Anglophile. Particular objections were raised to his delineation of India in a patronizing manner. Passages like the following in particular have raised the hackles of many an Indian nationalist critic:

> In India physical beauty is largely associated with a fair complexion or what we regard as such, and this among a people who are generally dark attracts attention immediately. (Part II Chapter I)

> The proportion of handsome women being somewhat low in India outside the Punjab, the women who are considered beautiful or who consider themselves beautiful are very self-conscious. They never allow anybody to overlook them. (Part II Chapter I)

> The dominant class in India is very paradoxical in one thing: it will never give any well-paid job to anyone who has not been educated or trained in the west. (Part II Chapter VII)

> In our society, an official of middle-class origins not only does not carry his brief case, he does not even take a paper to a colleague, he rings for the peon. This peon, on his part, will carry papers and files, but no packages. (Part II Chapter VII)

> The English Middle class is much more simple and general than we are. (Part II Chapter VII)

> Even in the big cities, for every two persons in clean and adequate clothing there are eight in an assortment of shabby, dirty, insufficient, and tattered clothes. In the cold season, as I travel in the public transport of Delhi, I often have sitting by my side men who

> have wrapped themselves with dirty blankets or quilts in which to all apperance they have been sleeping for years. In the villages, it is virtually impossible to meet men in clean and adequate clothing. (Part III Chapter III)

Surprisingly enough, many Indian critics have taken umbrage at Chaudhuri's observations. It would be preposterous to conclude that Chaudhuri is disparaging India before England. These are the differences that would quite naturally and automatically strike any one when one is faced with two diametrically opposite cultures. What Chaudhuri says about India in all the above instances is very nearly true and one can easily see eye to eye with his views. This does not, however, mean that we have to swallow all that Chaudhuri tells us in his book. Far from that, we cannot accept certain sweeping statements he makes in the books without a pinch of salt. For instance, the following statements are unconvincing generalizations:

> Religion and civilization were still interwoven with each other in England, as indeed in the west as a whole. (Part III Chapter V)

> In England the so-called upper classes were more religious than the common people. While in India the situation is exactly the opposite. (Part III Chapter V)

One cannot swallow these statements without questioning their validity.

Critics have placed Chaudhuri cheek by jowl with V.S. Naipaul, the author of *An Area of Darkness*. Both of them have been unduly accused of giving a morbid picture of India to the world. The image of India as it is projected in Chaudhuri's *A Passage to England* is quite different from that of *An Area of Darkness*. It must be conceded that Chaudhuri's portrayal of India is, by and large, realistic though unpalatable to most nationalist Indians.

Nayantara Sahgal's *The Day in Shadow*: A Feminist Perspective

T. ASOKA RANI

Feminism is an expression which connotes a movement for securing equality between the sexes in all walks of life, social, economic and political. It aims at ensuring for womanhood freedom in all respects. Feminist is a person, male or female, who is concerned with the status of women, and who advocates or works for the removal of all forms of discrimination and oppression of women so that they may live in a milieu of freedom, dignity and equality with men. Viewed from this angle, *The Day in Shadow* can truly be identified as a feminist novel and its writer, Nayantara Sahgal, as a feminist writer.

It is an indisputable fact that Nayantara Sahgal deals primarily with political themes in her novels. Nevertheless, her projection of woman's struggle for freedom and self-realization in her fiction cannot be lost sight of. She infuses into her heroines the spirit of self-respecting individualism. Her heroines always try to realize their selfhood either unconsciously as in the case of the earlier heroine like Kusum (*A Time to be Happy*) or consciously and deliberately, as in the case of her later heroines like Saroj (*Storm in Chandigarh*) and Simrit (*The Day in Shadow*).

In spite of her predilection for women's liberation, her brand of feminism does not reach out to the aggressive dimensions of gender-consciousness as reflected in the works of her western counterparts. She displays a very special kind of Indian sensibility. In *The Day in Shadow*, she shows how a woman can be criminally exploited 'without creating a ripple.'

Women's movement in the West has influenced the Indian feminist thinking to a large extent. But the model of the new woman suggested by the Western feminists is not acceptable in its entirety, given the conditions and sensibilities of Indian womanhood. Criticism levelled against Indian women writers, in general, is that they break down the orthodox model but fail to suggest a replacement model. It is remarkable that Nayantara Sahgal has a replacement model to offer, one based on protest. Chaman Nahal has all appreciation for her: "All her novels talk about women who are oppressed by marriage, by political circumstances, by accidents of history. They try to break out of that shell . . . particularly *The Day in Shadow* is a very good feminist novel. Within the limitation . . . women try to establish a model."[1]

In *The Day in Shadow*, the consummate thoroughness with which the novelist deals with the predicament of Simrit, a hapless divorcee in the male-dominated Indian society, prompts S.K. Tikoo to comment thus: "The novelist's unflagging concentration on Simrit's mental anguish, the quiet struggle that she wages and her continued fight till the end gives the novel the veritable aspect of feminist fiction."[2] Simrit is an independent woman who can make choices. She marries Som, solely attracted by his 'colour, life and action' disregarding the opposition from her parents and the dislike of her friends. Very soon, she realises her folly when she is forbidden in his house to have a say even in routine matters like choosing servants or a cook, selecting curtains or sofa-covers. Disillusioned at Som's attempts to restrict her personality and at the humiliating treatment meted out to her, Simrit resolves to dissolve her seventeen-year-old marriage. Even as a divorcee, she asserts her individuality. In defiance of the outworn traditions, she chooses to start life anew with Raj.

Simrit's concept of freedom cannot be mistaken for mere political or economic independence. It is a way of doing things one believes to be right and thus assert one's individuality. She is disappointed to realise that there is no place for free communication of ideas, friendship and partnership in the world of Som, dominated by overweening ambition and money. This denial of freedom leads her to a state of suffocation. Som's growing obsession with power and wealth, his opinion of Simrit as an object fit only for physical pleasure naturally lead to gradual estrangement between them.

Simrit finds herself shut out of Som's world. He never consults her in any matter. "Her usefulness to him had never extended to areas of the mind."[3] Unable to withstand his 'spiralling mania for affluence,' she longs to isolate herself from his world of commerce. All her attempts to change him go awry. Som becomes furious at her protests and asks her either to be a docile wife or to finish off the whole farce of their marital relationship. Simrit plumps, though reluctantly, for the second atternative. She is prepared to forsake him and all the riches and comforts rather than lead the abject life of a sex-satisfying companion. To live with self-respect is her primary preorgative and for that, she risks the unknown future with courage and confidence. She demonstrates that individual freedom is so precious that it should not be compromised or allowed to be suppressed.

It's common knowledge how difficult it is for an Indian woman to walk out of her husband's life. The women confronted with such a situation, the novelist, in an interview, observes: "They do not struggle in the radical sort of way recognized as struggle in the West. Yet they experience an even greater struggle to my mind, because they are coming out of much deeper roots and they endure to the utmost. When at last they can't take any more they make no bones about leaving, about doing what has to be done. They do not stay to remain slaves at that point. They go."[4] That's exacly what Simrit does. She dissolves her long marriage only when her attempts at safeguarding it prove futile. She proposes to Som to be friends without dissolving their marriage. He repudiates it with contempt. If Simrit does it, in spite of her large number of children, it is but a proof of her indomitable courage and strength of conviction in realising the goals she has set for herself.

After discarding her former role as an intellectual and a prolific writer, Simrit thinks she has a different and responsible role to play as a divorcee, feeling uprooted and abandoned in the society. Her problems encompassing physical, emotional and economic spheres are many and varied. A woman used to the luxuries of life—tastefully furnished accommodation and what not—suddenly finds herself to have to go without a telephone, even a milk or ration card. she has taken "all the living wealth [children] . . . and had left behind the crockery and furniture and linen and jewels and silver. . . . Som got all the things, the cars, the bank accounts." (58) While Som lives in luxury, Simrit lives in penury. She is not even sure how long her flat would be affordable, its rent being too expensive for her. In spite of all these problems, the courage with which she tries to adjust herself to the aftermath of the divorce is admirable.

Simrit possesses extraordinary will-power. As a single parent of her children, even in the most trying situations, she does not lose courage. She continues to be assertive and if the situation demands, even becomes aggressive. Her husband, too, is aware of her strength: "Som could have forgiven her if she had been a weaker being, unsure, dependent, even deceiving. But that beneath her docility she was none of these things was unpardonable." (53)

Moolchand, Som's company lawyer, at a meeting to clarify the Consent Terms to Simrit, finds it rather unbelievable for a woman to have absolute control over herself. The novelist writes: "Moolchand might have reacted better if she had broken down and wept, pleaded her plight, not displayed this control and competence. She was something outside his experience, a woman who exercised her mind." (59)

Simrit withstands the emotional trauma of her son's inclination towards her husband's commercial world with considerable equanimity. Raj too is full of admiration for her strength of mind. He understands: "She was basically tough, with the toughness of undivided integrity. And she was in his view exceptional for a woman. . . . No one who did not, could have moved bag and baggage from a whole past—with all those children. The prospect was intimidating." (38)

The most glorious instance of her self-confidence and crisis management is seen when she rejects with contempt Som's offer to receive the income that accrues of the shares on the condition of remaining unmarried. However, in spite of all her courage and strength, Simrit is admittedly passive. However, the writer does not consider it a weakness. She tells an interviewer: "Simrit is a passive yet not a weak heroine. She has a kind of strength out of her passivity."[5]

Simrit's signing of the document 'consent terms' is prone to attack, for she 'won't know where she is signing.'[6] She is trapped under the burden of the brutal divorce settlement cleverly drawn by Som to save his taxation which is 'worse than a life sentence.' (40) Her fault is to expect fair play in the deal and to sign it innocently and unsuspectingly. It shows, on the other hand, the essential callousness of Som, an image of the inhumanity of the patriarchal society. Simrit cannot believe that her husband could be so 'revengeful' and do this 'butchery' to her. She reflects: "No one treats another person like that, even when forgiveness is impossible." (53)

Simrit's acceptance of Raj as her husband comes under heavy attack. Nayantara Sahgal reacts sharply when an interviewer remarks that Simrit's break-up with Som turns out to be a joke towards the end when she accepts Raj as her man and thereby loses readers' sympathy and admiration:

> No, I certainly do not agree with this explanation. Perhaps you get baffled when Simrit finds happiness with a man, maybe because you are an orthodox male who resents such a development in a woman's life. I personally do not believe a woman has to be a martyr to prove her goodness.[7]

Her acceptance of Raj is based on his endearing qualities of tenderness, honesty and equality which she has vainly searched for in Som. Raj's 'rich warm concern' appeals to her and "he always did what he said he would do, the only stable element in the emotional debris of her new world." (16) He helps her regain her emotional and intellectual equilibrium.

Raj is a mature person, takes personal interest in her and loves her. The fact that she is a middle-aged woman with several children does not deter him. He has great respect for her and intends no foolery, "No handholding games with her. No games of any sort. With her it had to be on a long, strong basis." (157) His interest in her mainly springs from his passion for crusading against oppression of any kind.

Raj-Simrit relationship begins with the mind and not the body. They seek fulfilment not as possessions but as individuals. Listening to Raj, Simrit feels that she is lifted out and soothed. She muses: "After all attraction had to start somewhere and what better starting point than the mind?" (160) Ramkrishan perceives 'the fatal combine of love and friendship' in their relationship. He knows that physical love alone cannot sustain a relationship unless to it is added a milder food of friendship. Only friendship can last long and he sincerely believes that Raj and Simrit "would enjoy even a distance between them." (182) Simrit is aware that in marrying Raj, there is every possibility that her physical as well as psychological needs are met without losing her dignity and sense of equality and that she can live a truer life without any pretence:

> The personal world of Raj and Simrit, grounded in sympathy and understanding, human communication and friendship, rather than bestial sensuality and cruel insensitivity, seems to be the world that Nayantara not only wishes to depict but also prescribes as the only sane and sensible alternative to the machinistic world of power, atrocities and greed.[8]

In the process of emancipation, it has become necessary for Simrit to get rid of her fears and inhibitions. She has to overcome social opinion and orthodoxy on the one hand and personal hesitation and reluctance on the other. She continues to think, despite divorce, that her connection with Som is continued through her children and hence is besieged by feelings of guilt at her association with Raj. When Simrit meets Som to discuss the Consent Terms, Som's meanness comes before her in full proportions and perhaps this is the reason of her sudden feeling of being liberated from guilty feeling. She announces to Raj: "I'd got rid of my guilt. It was gone without a trace and in its place there was a strong, positive feeling." (208)

Raj too has been very hesitant and uncertain in his feelings towards Simrit before he becomes aware of his love for her. Simrit and her problems occupy his mind all the time. He ponders over the extent and depth of his attachment for her. Generally very assertive and domineering, he seems to hold back, sometimes deliberately also, when it comes to Simrit: "It was not a question of Simrit for himself—at least not until he had some sign from her. It was Simrit for himself he wanted, Simrit to forsake her shadows and begin to live." (167) When the sign comes from Simrit herself, there is nothing for Raj to hold back his love for her.

Their relationship is not one where Raj is domineering and dictating. There are several instances to show that there is perfect equality and, as a matter of fact, very often it is Simrit who takes decisions and imposes them on him. Simrit turns down Raj's proposal to have dinner in a hotel and "Raj accepted defeat." (14) Another time, Raj's proposal to have coffee at a restaurant is negatived and she suggests, instead, going to her house. Raj concedes, "All right, let's go. With you I face a dead end at every turn, unlike Som who must have ridden roughshod and triumphant. Did he?" (157) Apart from these matters of lighter vein, even in serious issues, in spite of her good opinion in his intellect, Simrit does not blindly listen to Raj. He is against her meeting Moolchand, Som's company lawyer. But Simrit decides and hence goes ahead. Even Raj recognises her independent spirit: "Her new life had nothing to do with him or any man. She could be that rarity, a woman with a profession, an independent person living her own life. She didn't need a man for identity or status." (139) Simrit's futile cry for equality in her relationship with Som materialises now in her relationship with Raj. Not legislation but understanding, love and respect can bring equality in a relationship and the fact that both of them have these qualities in abundance prompts Jasbir Jain to remark that their's "is an involving and an equal one."[9] Along with Raj, she builds up a world on the foundations of justice, equality and humanity. This novel thus "marks the emergence of the new type of woman who can present her own terms on which harmonious and dignified family life may be possible now and in future."[10]

It may not be fair to suppose that Simrit has left Som only when she has been sure of another man's help. Simrit has visited Raj after Som's ultimatum, but has not disclosed anything. Even to Raj's question, "Is there anything I can do?" she shook her head quickly, recovering herself and got up. (108)

It is very obvious that she has not even discussed her divorce issue with Raj. He had not seen the 'Consent Terms' till after the divorce. Simrit even tells Raj that had she known him during the trying period with Som, she might not have thought of divorce at all. "If I'd known you well before my divorce, there might not have been any divorce. Knowing you would have taken care of one need and my marriage another." (159) It shows that Raj's involvement in her divorce is a remote possibility.

Though Simrit loves Raj, she is not prepared to marry him, at least till her problems are solved. But Raj is particular that they should marry immediately so that he can share her problems and make her happy. Simrit is a middle-aged divorcee without money but several children and a tax problem, the size of a python. Hence no motives can be attributed to Raj's eagerness other than love for her and when she too loves him, he doesn't find any reason to prolong the relationship without the sanctity of marriage.

It may be justified to say that Simrit "hasn't even begun to see that she is a victim."[11] Simrit and Som's relationship is makred by lack of tenderness and warmth, communication and compatibility.

Hurt and humiliated at his condescending attitude, she suffers in silence for seventeen long years mainly because of her upbringing in a patriarchal society where male superiority is taken for granted. Her anxiety and restlessness are evident right from the beginning. "Simrit's quietness is restraint, not of quiescence; her silence a mark not of acceptance but of disagreement."[12] Her seeking divorce from Som is an indication of her protest against being victimized by him.

By accepting Raj, it should not be considered that Simrit continues to be a victim in the male-dominated society. Raj is a total contrast to Som—sensitive, warm and tender. He treats her as an equal and she is prefectly at ease in Raj's company.

Feminism is no doubt pro-woman but it neet not be anti-man. The novelist does not advocate 'female enclaves' and is not anti-male. She believes that a woman can fulfil herself wholly in the loving and harmonious relationship with a man. "Nayantara Sahgal's Simrit survives, though not entirely on her own terms, in an imperfect world where no one, not even man, can live entirely on his or her own terms."[13]

Women can be proud of their womanhood without developing antipathy towards men who have of necessity to play a supporting role as when fathers, brothers and husband reach out to the womenfolk. Such an inter-sex scenario will make for harmonious social environment. K.K. Sharma very appropriately says: "If feminism is based on the wrong attitude of hostility towards man, it will fizzle out, for the two genders are not only complementary and supplementary to each other but also absolutely indispensable for each other for full growth and fulfilment."[14]

If the ultimate goal of feminism is to make woman have freedom of choice and to live a life of her own, Simrit precisely exercises this freedom of choice in choosing Som earlier and Raj later. Raj appears to be superior to Simrit in intellect and therefore domineering in nature.

But Simrit with her independent spirit will never bow down before male authority. Perhaps, Nayantara Sahgal wants to bring home the essential truth that no man-woman relationship can exist on the principle of perfect equality. It is for a woman to have freedom and independence to lead an honourable and dignified life. There cannot be any doubt of Simrit possessing this in abundance.

"If the refusal to be crushed, the attempt to fight and voice protest is the core of feminism,"[15] Simrit is an embodiment of it. By bringing to the forefront her struggle for liberty, eqality, compatibility and self-reliance, *The Day in Shadow* becomes a feminist text in the truest sense of the term. Nayantara Sahgal proves her credentials as an impressive feminist writer by portraying Simrit as one who gives up her intolerably subservient role to vindicate her independence and self-respect and readjusts herself in her new role with dignity and responsibility.

NOTES

1. 'Feminism in English Fiction: Forms and Variations,' *Feminism and Recent Fiction in English,* ed. Sushila Singh (New Delhi: Prestige, 1991), 19.
2. *"The Day in Shadow:* An Experiment in Feminist Fiction," *Indian Women Novelists,* ed. R.K. Dhawan (New Delhi: Prestige, 1993) Set II, Vol. IV, 240.
3. Nayantara Sahgal, *The Day in Shadow* (Delhi: Vikas, 1976), 77.
4. Minoli Salgado, *Wasafiri*, 20 (1994), 44.
5. V. Mohini, "Writer at Work," *The Literary Criterion*, 25.1 (1990), 68.
6. Jaidev, "Problematizing Feminism," *Feminism and Recent Fiction in English*, ed. Sushila Singh, 59.
7. Shyam M. Asnani, "Interview with Nayantara Sahgal," *Punjab Journal of English Studies*, 5 (1990), 34.
8. Shyam M. Asnani, *Critical Response to Indian English in Fiction* (Delhi: Mittal, 1985), 130.
9. *Nayantara Sahgal* (New Delhi: Arnold Heinemann, 1978), 60.
10. S.K. Tikoo, 240.
11. Jaidev, 60.
12. Urbashi Barat, "Feminism in *The Day in Shadow*: Archetypal Patterns and Interpersonal Relationships," *Feminism and Literature*, ed. K.K. Sharma (Delhi: K.K. Publications, 1996), 75.
13. *Ibid.*, 79.
14. K.K. Sharma, "Feminism: Some Observations," *Feminism and Literature*, 201.
15. K. Meera Bai, "Feminism as an Extension of Existentialism: Woman in Indian English Fiction," *The Commonwealth Review*, 6:1 (94-95), 139.

Anita Desai's *Cry, the Peacock*: The Triumph of the Philosophy of Flux

RAVI NANDAN SINHA

Anita Desai's fiction attests the validity of the Heracleitian doctrine that all living is essentially flux, and what is generally called 'being' is merely a change from one state of consciousness to another. Her distinctive stature as a novelist derives primarily from the fact that she has made extensive use of the stream-of-consciousness technique in her novels. G. Rai puts the matter definitively: "She is almost alone among Indo-Anglian writers who has used stream-of-consciousness technique in her novels and short stories to explore the workings of the Indian mind."[1] The use of the internal monologue, manipulation of time and the use of symbolism as an exploratory device are some of the characterizing features of the stream-of-consciousness novel. A study of Anita Desai's first novel *Cry, the Peacock* can establish her preference for these devices.

In a limited sense, *Cry, the Peacocok* seems to deviate from Virginia Woolf's dictum that a novel is a record of an "ordinary mind on an ordinary day."[2] Anita Desai's characters have far from ordinary minds, if by ordinary we mean normal or commonplace. Maya in *Cry, the Peacock* and Monisha in *Voices in the City* are women who are trapped in one sense and free in another. They do not appear to represent the ordinary womanhood. They are trapped in certain states of the mind which force ordinary experience into neurotic moulds. Monisha is estranged from the family she lives in because she feels that they have "indoor minds."[3] Maya who experiences "hardly any love"[4] is not able to free herself from her past. In another sense, these women are free. They find it easy to escape the pull of the present and to roam freely in reflections, dream and images of desire. Maya and Monisha represent a class of unusual women. They are intelligent, intensely sensitive, obsessed and inexorably in love with themselves.

Despite the fact Maya and Monisha do not have 'ordinary' minds, the novels they appear in are about ordinary days in their lives. The reader is allowed to peep into the 'luminous halo' that life is and the internal monologue becomes an instrument of that revelation. Anita Desai makes use of the internal monologue in the same sense as Edouard Dujardin, the French novelist whom James Joyce singled out as the originator of the internal monologue, outlined,

> The internal monologue, like every monologue, is the speech of a given character, designed to introduce us directly into the internal life of this character, without the author's intervening by explaining or commenting, and like every monologue, is a discourse without a listener and a discourse unspoken; but it differs from the traditional monologue in that:
>
> as regards its substance, it expresses the most intimate thoughts, those closest to the unconsciousness;
>
> as regards its spirit, it is discourse before any logical organization reproducing thought in its original state and as it comes into the mind;
>
> as for its form, it is expressed by means of direct sentences reduced to a syntactic minimum;
>
> thus it responds essentially to the conception which we have today of poetry.[5]

Cry, the Peacock has passages of internal monologue which respond "essentially to the conception which we have today of poetry." Maya is a highly strung woman who feels the pressure of childhood memories and finds her conjugal life unsatisfactory. She is obsessed with death and since she is the central consciousness in the novel, it is appropriate that the novel should begin with a description of the death of her dog, Toto. She is in a state of severe shock and helplessness; the death of her pet keeps haunting her, "But she would not lift her face from a cushion, for fear of the stench of decaying flesh still hung in the bougainvillaea coloured evening air. All day it had come in with slow breeze that sucked the curtains in, then slowly drew them out. All day the purple flowers of the bougainvillaeas had cast a flood of coloured shade on her skin; it had been like warm blood bathing her, and could not be washed away." (6) The passage, besides revealing the inner Maya, has the concentration and sharpness of poetry.

In Part Two, there is a shift in the mode of narration. The first person narrative is used for the first time. The point of view is Maya's. Beginning with the death of her pet, Maya's thoughts spiral into the various aspects of her relationship with her husband, Gautama. Her thoughts, she says, "rose, every now and then, like birds that awake from dreams and rise out of their trees amidst great commotion, circle a while, then settle again, on other branches." (21) In the stream of her consciousness, memories and impressions mingle. Her mind flits from her pet to Gautama and back:

> Something slipped into my tear hazed vision, a shadowy something, that prodded me into admitting that it was not my pet's death alone that I mourned today but another sorrow, unremembered, perhaps as yet not experienced, and filled me with this despair. . . . Lying on my bed with my eyes shut, I tried to think—of the dog rolling over on his back to gaze at me with fond, flower-soft eyes—was it that? Ah, now that I thought of it, it was, it was indeed, I insisted, clenching my fingers about the pillow. But the pillow, Gautama's was hard, did not relent, forced me to admit that the strange horror had not yet been recognized even though it was, surely, connected with the corpse and the small, soft corpse and the odour of flesh, once sweet, once loved, then, suddenly, rotten, repulsive. And the liquid brightness of the mirror blurred, the picture went out of focus, I crept into a corner of the bed, crouched there, thinking that it was perhaps because of Gautama not understanding. (8)

At the subliminal level, Maya equates the soft, decaying carcass of her dog with the decay of her relationship with Gautama.

William Troy used the term 'superior Bohemia' in his discussion of the novels of Virginia Woolf and said that her novels are peopled with characters whose experience is largely vicarious and whose contact with actuality is incomplete. For Maya too, 'actuality' presents a distorted image. She often plays truant into the past. Breakfast in the garden with her father was "as good as a revel of elves and fairies who feast on melons and syrups by moonlight." (43) There are hidden terrors in the past: the figure of the albino which haunts her constantly and the unsettling memory of the Sikh who talked of fate. Maya appears to be cracking slowly:

> Not only their words, but their fate. And now, once more, I strained to hear them calling on the Ridge, that rocky wasteland—a romantic hideout of storms, sunsets, wilderness—that crosses old Delhi, and is peopled with rabbits and porcupines, and the snakes and peacocks of my childhood, as well as burning Flame of the Forest trees and secret robber caves and crumbling Moghul ruins. Had I heard one, I believe I should have expired, for my

> heart was so stretched with fear, that one small droplet of sound in it would have strained it to bursting. Listened to it pound, and twisted on my bed, crying the peacock's cry. And I knew I should never again sleep in peace. For God, now I was caught in the net of the inescapable, and where lay the possibility of mercy, of release? This net was no hallucination, no. In the day-time, amidst companions, I could force myself into believing that it was only a nightmare, no more. But, in the night, under the stark gaze of the moon, in that waiting silence, my memories came to life, were so vivid, so detailed, I knew them to be real, too real. Or, is it madness? Am I gone insane? Father! Brother! Husband! Who is my saviour? I am in need of one. I am dying, and I am in love with living. I am in love, and I am dying. God, let me sleep, forget, rest. But no, I'll never sleep again. There is no rest anymore—only death and waiting. (97-98)

The novelist's task, Virginia Woolf believed, is to convey the essential character, to convey "this unknown and uncircumscribed spirit" with whatever aberration or complexity it may have "with as little mixture of the alien and external as possible."[6] Brilliantly poetic passages of internal monologue scattered throughout the novel reveal the essential Maya. Prema Nandakumar calls Maya a character "caught in her own despair (having) Proustian undertones."[7] To illustrate:

> Rats will suckle their young most tenderly. I know this, as now I lived quite near one, with seven young ones nestling between her legs. It may seem strange, incredible, yet no stranger than that the god whirling upon the torchlit stage steps down, flings away the mask of virdian green and dead white, flings it away quite gracelessly, and reveals himself as an aged monkey, going flabby now, and perspiring, so that a foul stench surrounds him. And the god who leaps and whirls by torchlight, rules over the four cornered *diva* with its flickering copper flames, and the aged monkey, hairy about the ears, are one. He even clears his throat and spits. But then, long ago I knew of snakes that coil themselves around the sweet-smelling sandalwood trees of the forest. Queen of the night attracts snakes too, and tube roses. All white flowers, chaste sweet white flowers, luring the snakes to their hearts of scent. And they come, the snakes, they come slithering towards these virgins of the night, with only their small cold eyes glinting in the dark, and they cling to the bending stalk, and with forked tongues lash and lash again at the heart of innocence. One never knows but one may

> bend to look into the yellow pollen upon a fragile stamen and be struck between the eyes, deeply and fatally, by a viper's fang. One never knows but one may applaud a dancer and then find him a perspiring, asthmatic, flapjawed ape. And the rats with their young, suckling them, then lashing their tails, spreading plague. One must be careful for one never knows. Careful then, oh doubly, triply careful. (126-27)

The flow of consciousness from rats to a god "whirling upon the torchlit stage" to snakes and then "the sweet smelling sandalwood trees of the forest" is rapid. Andre Gide wrote in his notebook (17 June, 1919), "Never present *ideas* except in terms of temperaments and characters."[8] Maya is an idea as much as a temperament. She is a self divided between the past and the present, between security and terror. As the novel unfolds, the border line between reality and dream, between sanity and insanity is gradually obliterated. Madhusudan Prasad underlines this fact when he says, "Desai ably explores the turbulent emotional world of the neurotic protagonist Maya."[9] Ramesh Kumar Srivastava also suggests, "The plot of the novel is woven of three broad strands which cause Maya's psychic turmoil: her obsession with death, her father fixation and her incompatible relationship with Gautama as also the resultant alienation."[10] Maya's childhood is dominated by the figure of her father who is a constant presence in the novel. Without pushing the parallels too close, it can be suggested that like Mrs. Ramsay in Virginia Woolf's *To the Lighthouse*, Maya's father is a lingering presence even when he is not there. Gautama is unable to become her father's emotional substitute because Maya is too immature to accept him as he is. In her mind, there is also the stalking fear caused by the albino's prediction that in the fourth year of their marriage either Maya or Gautama will die. To this is added the ever present fear of insanity. Maya's is a desperate attempt to hold on to sanity when "memories come to life, were so vivid, so detailed, I knew them to be real, too real. Or is it madness?" (97-98) The disintegration of her personality is complete when she kills Gautama by pushing him over the parapet and finally goes insane.

In a stream-of-consciousness novel, imagery and symbolism play a central role and *Cry, the Peacock* is no exception. The dog Toto's death evokes the image of molten lead, "Now and then she went out into the verandah, and looked to see if he were coming up the drive which lay shrivelling, melting and then shrivelling again like molten lead in a groove cut into the earth." (5-6) In her present state of shock, the world presses upon her with the heaviness of lead. The image of lead evokes both weight and poison. Images related to lead are frequently employed in the novel. To give just one example, "dark blobs of flotsam floating on a leaden sea." (172) Images related to disease and hospital abound in the novel:

> . . . the sun hung pendent . . . like . . . a purulent boil, until it was ripe to drop. (6)
>
> [Gautama did] all that was to be done quickly and quietly like a surgeon's knife at work. (6)
>
> . . . it had been like warm blood bathing her and could not be washed away. (6)
>
> The light merely turned red, tinged with my own blood that crept through the hair-fine veins across my lids. I saw the world through my own blood that morning, and it was red. (182)

These images suggest Maya's pervert fascination with death.

To Maya "the central lingam was painted a bright viscious red as though plunged in sacrificial blood." (28) The colour red and all that it brings to mind symbolizes an acute egocentricism. Red and brown are colours of individuality because they suggest the colour of blood and that of the human body whereas blue and green are colours of impersonality because they stand for the earth and the sky. Most of the images in the novel evoke the red or pink colour because they objectify Maya's nameless fear of death and her obsession with herself.

Images of violence and animals are equally common in *Cry, the Peacock*. The dance of the peacock is an image of central importance in the novel. "'Pia, pia' they cry. 'Lover, lover. Mio, mio,—I die, I die.' . . . How they love the rain—these peacocks. They spread out their splendid tails and begin to dance, but, like Shiva's, their dance of joy is the dance of death, and they dance, knowing that they and their lovers are all to die." (95) The image of a Kathakali dance, the moon as "the fierce dancer," (28) all symbolize violence and death. To conclude with one more example:

> Will it be fire? Will it be flood?
>
> Will the lizards rise out of the desert to come upon us—either upon him or upon myself—with lashing tails and sliding tongues, to crush us beneath their bellies?
>
> Will there be blood? Will there be screams?
>
> And when? When? (179)

The apparent contradiction between the flux and the fixity of life has been resolved well by Anita Desai. *Cry, the Peacock* resembles Virginia Woolf's *The Waves* in intensity and poetic quality but Desai's novel does not have many modulations of perspective. It is centered in one consciousness, that of Maya and it is possible to regard Gautama as a part of Maya's emotional environment. Maya's attempts to reach out to Gautama can be interpreted as Maya's efforts to come to terms with a truth outside herself. She fails in this attempt because success would have meant surrendering the uniqueness of her ego to an impersonal reality. The achievement of Anita Desai lies in the fact that she employs a relatively new technique in Indian English fiction with such consummate skill.

NOTES

1. "The Soil and the Roots: A Study of the Novels of Anita Desai," *The Indian Novel in English*, ed. Ravi Nandan Sinha (Calcutta: Ankit, 1987), p. 93.
2. Virginia Woolf, *Common Reader*, First Series, p. 189.
3. Anita Desai, *Voices in the City* (Delhi: Orient Paperbacks, 1955), p. 139.
4. Anita Desai, *Cry, the Peacock* (Delhi: Orient Paperbacks, 1980), p. 108.
5. Qtd. Leon Edel in *The Psychological Novel* (London: Rupert Hart-Davies, 1955), pp. 53-54.
6. Virginia Woolf, *Common Reader*, First Series.
7. *Indian Literature since Independence* (New Delhi: Sahitya Akademi, 1973), p. 57.
8. *The Counterfeiters with Journal of 'The Counterfeiters'* (New York: Alfred A. Knopf, 1951), p. 374.
9. *Anita Desai: The Novelist* (Allahabad: New Horizon, 1981), p. 32.
10. *Six Indian Novelists in English* (Amritsar: Guru Nanak Dev University, 1987), p. 279.

Superstition and Psyche in Anita Desai's *Cry, the Peacock*

M. RAJESHWAR

Maya, the central character of Anita Desai's *Cry, the Peacock*,[1] is obsessed almost from the beginning of the novel with the gloomy prophecy of an albino astrologer. According to the prophecy, she or her husband would die during the fourth year of her marriage. Her father dismisses the prophecy as nonsense and orders that it should be forgotten. Obeying his wish, Maya keeps the prophecy rigorously repressed in her unconscious until her marriage with Gautama enters the fourth year. Now triggered off by the death of her pet dog, Toto, it assumes during the course of the novel the shape of an obsessional neurosis and keeps gnawing at the core of her being like an oversized pest feeding on a tender leaf.

It is strange that Maya should so superstitiously believe in the veracity of the prophecy although she knows that Gautama and his family "hoot with derision at the mention of superstition." (75-76) In the beginning of her neurotic affliction she frequently tells herself that it was she herself who was fated to die. But she is in ardent love with life and so she soon begins to wonder whether it was not "Gautama's life that was threatened." (164) Taking this line of reasoning further she fears for her life and would keep the secret for herself at any cost. "He must not know, not even guess. Never, never, never. If he guessed, new dangers would arise like sudden fires out of the cracked earth. . . . Ah, if Gautama found out, would he, might he not put me in peril of my life? Did he not love life too." (151) Not very long after she is almost convinced that Gautama is certainly fated to die and the thought makes her more and more secretive. "I glanced at him now, slyly, for sly I had grown with such a load of secrets that had to he hidden from him, such evil and awful secrets." (165)

It has been suggested in the novel and later harped on by critics that Maya is obsessed with the prophecy because of the romance involved in it. But the knowledge of depth psychology holds the promise of examining her irrational and superstitious belief from an entirely new angle. Freud attributes superstitious beliefs to suppressed hostility.

> It can be recognized most clearly in neurotics suffering from obsessional thinking . . . that superstition derives from suppressed hostile and cruel impulses. Superstition is in large part the expectation of trouble; and a person who has harboured frequent evil wishes against others, but has been brought up to be good and has therefore repressed such wishes into the unconscious, will be especially ready to expect punishment for his unconscious wickedness in the form of trouble threatening him from without.[2]

Does Maya's superstition too originate in her suppressed hostile and cruel impulses? To all appearances she has been an absolutely submissive and obedient daughter, sister and wife and so it may sound outrageous to accuse her of harbouring cruel impulses. But probing into her unconscious would reveal that there is immense suppressed hostility in her unconscious against her husband and to an extent against her father.[3] Being a "creature of instinct" (16) she seems to hold Gautama responsible for her unfulfilled instinctuality in the marital relationship. She is also angry with him because after four years of life together, she is compelled to come to the sad conclusion that she would soon lose her already rudimentary self. She grows anxious on account of the threats to her self-preservation and neurotiocally perceives Gautama's death as a solution. The prophecy comes an a convenient external justification to her unconscious wish and for that reason she tenaciously clings to it. I will dwell at some length on Maya's reasons for wishing Gautama dead and then return to her superstitious belief.

Maya is extremely faithful to her instincts which, as is their nature, crave for unqualified and wild satisfaction. According to Freudian tenets, normal people in her circumstances would have effected a withdrawal by influencing the instinctual urges at the psychic level. But tragically for Maya, her very life appears to be intricately woven with and highly dependent on her instincts. Given her instinctuality Maya expects some emotional and physical satisfaction in married life but both of them are denied her, one by Gautama's cold intellectuality and the other by his age. Maya's longing for the sensuous enjoyment of life is dampened by liberal doses of the *Gita* philosophy of non-attachment. Her effusive emotionality is always counter-balanced by Gautama's analytical mind. While he views "nothing subjectively, nothing with passion" (150) she is "flooded with tenderness and gratitude" (11) when he merely touches her hair, falls "into the soft, velvet well of the primordium of original instinct, of first-formed love" (11) when he draws a finger down her cheek, and takes to hating her own pretty face for failing to make any impact on him. She has to thus continually contend with unreciprocated emotionality and feels terrible on that score.

Sex is not only an intensely and intrinsically pleasurable experience but it can act as a revitalising force in an otherwise sterile life. Freud, in fact, views sex as the prototype of all pleasurable experiences of life. Maya's earth-bound nature makes her well-inclined to derive the fullest satisfaction from this intimate exxperience. It is difficult to conjecture what course her psyche would have taken if she were married to a much younger man and had been satisfied sexually. But because of Gautama's age and attitude to sex she remains a much disappointed woman. Even when they do make love the act is utterly devoid of passion. Several passages in the novel have been devoted to the portrayal of her disillusionment in sex. At the beginning of the novel itself Maya makes a frank admission of her sexual dissatisfaction born of Gautama's unpardonable negligence. "Telling me to go to sleep while he worked at his papers, he did not give another thought to me, to either the soft, willing body or the lonely, wanting mind that waited near his bed." (9) Frustrated by his coldness she gives herself up to a fit of pillow-beating! As her disillusionment becomes a routine experience she increasingly sexualises her surroundings, perhaps by way of displacement. The papaya trees in the courtyard, for example, assume a new sexual significance for her. "I contemplated that, smiling with pleasure at the thought of those long streamers of bridal flowers that flow out of the core of the female papaya tree and twine about her slim trunk, and the firm, wax-petalled blossoms that leap directly out of the solid trunk of the male." (92) As her grip over herself begins to slacken she begins to experience hallucinatory visions of lizards and birds coupulating in weird settings.

> Of lizards, the lizards that come upon you, stalking you silently, upon clawed toes, slipping their clublike tongues in and out, in and out with an audible hiss . . . they have struck you to a pillar of salt which, when it is motionless they will mount and lash with their slime-dripping tongues, lash and lash again, as they grip with curled claws, rubbing their cold bellies upon yours, rubbbing and grinding, rubbing and grinding. (127)

What Maya experiences here seems to be a symbolic gratification of the sexual desire which remains unfulfilled in actual life.

The image of fighting and mating peacocks, apart from being the central motif of the novel, underlines Maya's sexual frustration too. The memory of her innocent enjoyment of their call in her childhood becomes a foil to her present over-crowded mind, full of bird and animal imagery. "But sleep was rent by the frenzied cries of peacocks pacing the rocks at night—peacocks searching for mates, peacocks tearing themselves to bleeding shreds in the act of love, peacocks screaming with agony at the death of love. The night sky turned to a flurry of peacocks' tails, each star a staring eye." (175) In spite of her total frustration, Maya's moral scrupulosity does not allow her to cross the bounds of marital morality. Nor is she able to sublimate this powerful biological urge in the manner of her friend Leila who selflessly serves her tuberculous husband. Her married life ends up being emotionally and socially sterile.

A continuous frustration of the body's sexual needs can be disastrous to somebody like Maya, given her fierce instinctuality. A healthy emotional and sexual life would have given her a sense of security and stopped her psyche from decaying. This view acquires validation from Freud's observation:

> experience shows . . . that women, who, as being the actual vehicles of the sexual interests of mankind, are only endowed in a small measure, with the gift of sublimating their instincts, and who . . . when they are subjected to the disillusionments of marriage, fall ill of severe neuroses which permanently darken their lives.[4]

Freud attributes neurosis of women to sexual dissatisfaction resulting from the rigours of civilized sexual morality. Biologically speaking, marital unfaithfulness could be a viable cure for the ailment. However, such a thing entails perhaps the most severe indictment in the rigidly organized Indian society. Freud continues:

> the more strictly a woman has been brought up and the more sternly she has submitted to the demands of civilization, the more she is afraid of taking this way out; and in the conflict between her desires and her sense of duty, she once more seeks refuge in a neurosis. Nothing protects her virtue as securely as illness. (47)

Maya too seeks a neurotic solution but only to find it inadequate. Something more drastic than neurosis needs to be considered by her psyche.

Secondly, Maya perceives that eventually she will lose her self as a result of a long experience of eventlessness. Her life appears to her as an endless tedium with nothing significant taking place at any time. She is never the centre of importance nor is she instrumental in any event.

The sphere of her social activities is so severely restricted that she seems to feel suffocated within it. But by Indian standards her life situation appears to be ideal. She has a secure home, earning husband and well-defined future. These seemingly ideal external conditions are however not acceptable to her unconscious where her desire for unbridled freedom is hidden.

The novel abounds in incidents that show how her longing for outdoor life is constantly frustrated mainly by Gautama. As a child she had enjoyed the scenic beauty and cool weather of Darjeeling and now she longs to go there with Gautama. When she timidly suggests the possibility to Gautama he replies in a cold astringent tone, "Why don't you? . . . Your father would take you wherever you wanted to go. He *can*." (40) The Kathakali ballets performed at night in parts of South India, hold great attraction to Maya.

> 'I want—I want, . . . to see the Kathakali dances. I have heard of the ballets they have in their villages. . . . And the dancers are all men. . . . The masks they wear—you must have seen them? And their costumes. And the special kind of music. And it is all our in the open, at night, by starlight—and perhaps they have torches. (42-3)

To her imploration to take her to the South, Gautama coolly suggests that she wait till a Kathakali troupe comes to Delhi. He apparently sees no strong reason to undertake a tiresome journey down South in the sweltering summer.

The fact of Maya's constricted life comes most vividly alive in the scene of Gautama's all-male party. Charmed by the vibratingly rich Urdu poetry recited by these cultured wine-drinking gentlemen, Maya breaks an age-old rule and joins them. While the other men politely, but uneasily, respond to her presence Gautama not only shatters her hope of participating in the pulsating and poetry-charged atmosphere but also subtly drives home to her the truth that she does not belong there.

> Turning his back to me, he stood talking to a friend, a glass in his hand, and his voice rose, in order that I might hear, when he said, 'Blissful, yes, because it is unrelated to our day, unclouded by the vulgarity of ill-educated men, or of overbearing women.' (104)

To add to her problems stemming from inactivity she remains childless. The birth of a child would have given her a sense of achievement and her creative urge would have got focussed on a helplessly dependent human being instead of getting diffused over nature and spread outside human interest.

Three plus years of married life and the prospect of a passionless and unchallenging life for the next forty or fifty years, during which she would continue to be obedient to her husband and face neither choices nor challenges, comes as a shocking revelation to her hyper-active mind. Her repeated confesssion that she or Gautama will surely die, in a way, indicates that the opposite would be true—that especially Gautama will not die before her. So according to this logic if she is to live and find the happiness that is her due Gautama will have to go. And the focal point of her thought, day in and day out, becomes the albino's prophecy which appears to justify and dramatise her wish. But she allows herself considerable time before she does anything drastic. All through the novel she keeps her wish hidden in her unconscious and the prophecy itself shrouded in secrecy. This is because as a neurotic she is still aware of the moral sanctions against such wishes. Indoctrinated to be faithful to her husband, she feels her hand held back by an invisible force. The neurotic defence mechanisms such as sleep rituals, hallucinatory visions and nightmares (where her secret longings come alive to her), experience of split personality, adverse somatic symptoms and religious avoidance of violence woefully fail to blunt the edge of her unconscious wish. At most places she appears to reel under the pressure and break to pieces as a result of the struggle within. Yet she hesitates. She is aware of the unseemly consequences and she is scared of not only society but her own conscience. In order to be done with Gautama without antagonising the social imperatives and her own super-ego the only way that is still open to her is psychosis. Once a human organism is entrusted to psychosis, nature takes its own course. The preservation of its physical integrity becomes more important than the protection of its social image. In fact, in psychotics the super-ego, the moral agency, becomes completely inactive. Psychosis would thus help Maya to carry out her wish without earning disapproval. She therefore progressively moves towards a psychotic solution to her struggle.

Her transition from neurosis to psychosis is powerfully underscored in the scene of the dust-storm in which she is shown as running "on and on, from room to room, laughing as maniacs laugh once the world gives them up and surrenders them to their freedom." (190) Maya's shutting herself in as a measure of protection from the raging dust-storm is symbolic of her total withdrawal from the world of purposeful action and meaningful relationships. The exact point of her plunging into the abysmal depths of psychosis, however, is her act of violence itself. Maya's pushing Gautama off the parapet of their house is not fortuitous. There are simply no accidents in psychic life. Behind Maya's final indulgence in violence there has been a prolonged psychic struggle which she has not known herself. Having done the deed and having taken recourse to psychosis she relaxes and openly declares that unlike her, Gautama has not been in love with life and so according to the prophecy he had to die. "It had to be one of us, you see, and it was so clear that it was I who was meant to live. You see, to Gautama it didn't really matter. He didn't care, and I did." (215-16) Governed by the primary process thinking, she does not camouflage her thoughts by drawing on her linguistic resources any more. Her adult life with all its responsibilities and anxieties has become a sealed book for her. She is faithful to herself and the social and moral consequences of her actions do not matter to her any more now.

Her superstitious belief thus helped her immensely in the process of unconsciously identifying her problems and their source. From a shadowy figure the albino sprang to life and has come to mean much to her during her neurotic struggle. After she embraced psychosis what the charlatan said years ago has become gospel truth to her. But for him she would not have perceived Gautama as her foremost enemy and would not have considered the possibility of violently working out her equation with him.

NOTES

1. (Delhi: Orient Paperbacks, 1980, rpt. 1988).
2. Sigmund Freud, "Determinism, Belief in Chance and Superstition—Some Points of View," *The Psychopathology of Everyday Life,* trans. Alan Tyson (Harmondsworth: Penguin, 1960), p. 232.
3. In an earlier article while playing down the father fixation theory I argued that Maya nursed a grouse against her father Raisahib for impeding the development of her individuality with his over-protective attitude all through her childhood and adolescence, then or throwing her into the fetters of marriage with a passionless and cold intellectual and finally for callously neglecting her thereafter. I concluded that Maya unconsciously took her revenge against him by creating a scandal which she knew he dreaded. But in psychological life things are 'over determined.' Every significant psychological event in a person's life has a multiplicity of reasons. Maya's wish to avenge herself on her father could be only one of the many reasons for her to want to kill Gautama. "Anita Desai's *Cry the Peacock*: The Father's Unconscious," *Indian English Literature Since Independence*, ed. Ayyappa Paniker (New Delhi: Indian Association for English Studies, 1991), pp. 44-48.
4. Sigmund Freud, *Civilized Sexual Morality and Modern Nervous Illness*, trans. James Strachey (Harmondsworth: Penguin, 1985), p. 47.

Anita Desai's *Journey to Ithaca*: A Quest for Integrated Being

MRINALINI SOLANKI

Anita Desai's novels reveal her persistent concern with the themes of anxiety, anguish and psychological adaptation necessitated by the threats to the individual's identity and relation to reality. She emphasizes certain other aspects also, which some individuals find significant in their social interaction, such as interpersonal relations, the ultimate reality, general futility in life, nothingness, worthlessness. Her protagonist's awareness of nothingness and futility in life burdens them with a tragic inability to relate to others in a spirit of love and mutual understanding. In her fictional world most of the human relationships are seen to suffer from acute breakdown of communication. Marital, filial, social and communal relations are locked in a kind of meaninglessness, empty rituals observed for the sake of convention, not leading the characters to any personal fulfilment or development.

Anita Desai's characters are burdened by their uniqueness. They want to exercise their freedom, make a choice and refuse to conform or compromise. All of them find the ordinary routine of life boring and disgusting. To accept life as it comes in routine is unauthentic existence for Anita Desai's protagonists. They all ask themselves the question whether there is not a way of life which they can follow with intellectual integrity and emotional conviction. Desai's female protagonists strive for harmony and fulfilment in human relationships whereas her male protagonists are dissatisfied with the practices which are repugnant to their conscience, with beliefs which are incredible in their character and do not command themselves to the sensitive minds. It is logical therefore that alienation acquires a broad significance and range of meaning in Anita Desai's novels. In sociological terms it means loneliness, the absence of relationships, the feeling of dissatisfaction or the explicit rejection of social values and norms. For Sartre, alienation is the individual's experience of himself as an object, which is not a disparity to be overcome, but a fact to be acknowledged.[1]

Anita Desai's latest novel, *Journey to Ithaca*, is a moving account of Matteo's nagging sense of alienation and his quest for spirituality. Like so many western youths in the sixties and seventies, the young Italian boy Matteo leaves his luxurious home and affluent family in search of something more and beyond his mundane existence. This he hopes to find in spiritual enlightenment in the ashrams of India. Detachment and alienation are inherent in his behaviour from the very beginning. Like a perennial outsider he is always lonely and ill at ease in the world in which he lives. His interest in the Indian religion becomes the sole object of his consciousness. For Matteo, religion is what Oswald Spengler says, "the first and last metaphysics, the other worldliness and a life with the supersensible."[2]

Matteo, a portrait of loneliness and alienation, learns an attitude of quiet resignation and non-acceptance in childhood only, when he always plays by himself. An introvert by nature he is neither free with anyone nor does he want to share his feelings with others. His answers to the questions of his parents are sullen and monosyllabic. His attempts to keep clear of others reveal his desire to escape from real life and his disgust with his immediate human context. On Sundays he runs out into a country along the sides at the dusty motor roads. "He runs for hours . . . brushing past people running and running."[3] Like Arun Joshi's Som Bhaskar in *The Last Labyrinth*, Matteo is always in a hurry like a hare chased by unseen sounds. The incomplete schooling creates problems for Matteo. Apart from job opportunities he is deprived of the most important aspect of social interaction at the different stages in school. Hugo in *Baumgartner's Bombay*, cut off from the outside world, is immensely attached to his mother but Matteo is not attached to either of his parents. "He stared at both of them and felt they repelled him equally. It seemed painful that they should be related." (19)

Matteo is withdrawn from the school. His father engages a tutor to teach him English. But his sudden spring like motion on looking at the title of his tutor's book, *The Journey to the East* by Herman Hesse, is the turning point in Matteo's life. He tries to quench his ravaging thirst by possession of an object, a book. Fabian, the tutor and Matteo become good friends as they understand each other's needs, "Matteo and Fabian were walking with an open book . . . throwing back their heads to shout to each other like two madmen." (21) With Fabian, Matteo's life becomes worth living. Interaction with him and a new-found feeling of belongingness provide strength and vigour to his thoughts and feelings. Fabian, in fact, turns out to be his friend, philosopher and guide. Fabian enters Matteo's life like a comet brightening his mind and leading him on to the celestial way to freedom at a very tender stage. His mother is aghast seeing the book in Matteo's hand "catching Matteo by his collar, the book in her hand. She marches into papa's room shouting, 'Will you see what this Englishman of yours has sent your son to read? . . . See if it is fit to place in the hands of a school boy?'" (26) Matteo is sick of his parents' involvement in his present and future. Each suggestion from them erects a barbed wire fence between the child and his parents. Locks and barriers become insignificant when he takes a flight from the filial bondages. "He would run and run as if all he wanted was to place a distance between them and himself, a distance he drew out to greater lengths with each run." (27)

Matteo's alienation and escape from his parents and community affect his matrimonial equation also. Due to ideological polarities, Matteo does not find satisfaction and happiness with his wife Sophie. She is unable to adjust to his way of life and thinking because he rates the world of Gurus as more real and true than the world of Sophie or his parents. Sri Aurobindo believes that in the state of "Superamental Manifestation, individuals have developed, what he calls, the mind of light, which is the last of a series of descending planes of consciousness in which the super mind or modification of its self manifests in activities."[4] Matteo thinks that by relating himself to the visions and insights of great sages he can have the first hand knowledge of ultimate truths. No wonder, Matteo finds an abysmal barrier between himself and the mundane world. He is unable to relate to the space around him. Space, in existential context, does not mean the physical area but "the human environment, and every other that provides the setting in which human life is to be lived."[5] He tells Sophie, "it is spiritual experience for which you must search in India, nothing less." (36) For him the meaning of spirituality is believing only what he sees. His escape or denial of reality shatters the mind of Sophie. A down to earth, materialistic and practical Sophie wants to keep the primary ties strong and asks her husband, "Why, Matteo, why? Why can we not be together again at home with the children?" (4) Like an ideal wife she wants that Matteo should stay away in Ashram after he recovers from his illness, "When you are well, Matteo we will leave." (4) The suggestion infuriates Matteo. Coleman rightly observes: "We tend to avoid those aspects of the situation which are traumatic or self devaluating or contradictory to our assumptions."[6]

Matteo gets lost in the mazes of blind faith. He thinks spirituality is something very easy to achieve. Wearing a faded and torn kurta pyjama and chappals, he feels himself close to the supreme power. This ignorance remains a bliss to him like hoards of other pilgrims he comes across at various holy places. Outwardly, he tries to do what the sadhus do on the sand banks of rivers. He is startled to see a Sadhu swimming across the river banks even when the river is in full spate. This needs *Sadhana* or a course of spiritual discipline. He has faith but fails to attain wisdom and contentment in spite of his best efforts to undertake the path of spiritual glory. Without proper training and knowledge, it is difficult for Matteo to be blessed with an encounter with the higher reality. "He had done with the travels, the crowds, the pilgrims, the talk, the drink, the smoke, the adventures. He had them too, had travelled and searched them out with others, but neither seen nor experienced what the others did." (64) His conflicts persist and the sense of integration seems to be nowhere near him. He is in the grip of disintegration within and without. The sense of exhilaration, that release of energy, the spirit that characterize liberty and freedom he fails to achieve.

Faith and meditation are the two skills needed to have a vision of spiritual truth. To have a whole-hearted devotion and concentration one needs lot of practice, discipline and self-sacrifice. Matteo's lack of faith in himself and in those around him makes him withdraw from the outside world. "He felt disabled, without the skills the others possessed, a kind of leper amongst them." (66) His search for eternal truth makes him vulnerable. His quest becomes the quest for survival. His life becomes so meaningless and worthless that without having a vision of spiritual truth, "It became impossible to return to the room, to the company of anyone." (67) In search of spiritual truth he embarks upon another journey. A temple on the way turns out to be an abode for a stone. The sight of an old man worshipping a stone makes him feel all the more confused and lost. To him it is nothing but a smooth, round stone. But soon he realizes the circle as the universe containing world within world, ring upon ring, sphere within sphere, "The stone glowed now, became brilliant in Matteo's eyes . . . he felt certain divine light." (68) This divine light helps him see the enormous complexity of human existence—a labyrinth within the labyrinth.

In a bid to unravel the mystery of this labyrinth, Matteo moves from Ashram to Ashram and from one Yogi to another but peace of mind and inner happiness elude him. All these futile ventures affect his health. Sophie takes pity on his condition and feels dismayed as his ridiculous predicament reminds her of "an insect that had become disoriented and lost its bearings." (70) J.G. Bennett has rightly observed: "What makes you panic is the inability to accept our own nothingness. It looks as if there is a darkness ahead of us and we are frightened of going into that darkness."[7]

Matteo's hunt is not yet over. From a magazine stall he is able to get a book entitled *The Mother*. The photograph of the Mother becomes an epitome of eternal bliss to him. Matteo reaches the Mother's ashram, his joy knows no bound on hearing the Mother speak to the devotees. For him it is the old woman's voice not the words but "the voice itself that gives all these natural phenomena a wonderful significance." (98) For the first time since his departure from Italy he experiences a sense of unity between the mundane and the divine. He describes to Sophie what he experienced of unity, "the unity of the spiritual with the physical, the dark with the light, the human with the natural." (99) Matteo feels further enlightened to hear the Mother speak about the Divine Light. The divine force is everywhere and knowledge means the realization of this truth. The Mother exhorts them all not to feel sad or exhausted but keep smiling. "The purpose of our existence in the ashram is to experience fully, my friend." (100) The Mother further preaches that without making an effort it is difficult to become a devotee. Since the Mother believes in the motto "Work is Worship," she assigns duties to all the devotees in the ashram and explains to them: "This effort, the endeavour, this exercise, it is Sadhana? If the artist performs this exercise, it is artistic. If the farmer performs it, it is spiritual and it all leads to Achievement." (102)

Matteo finds in the image of the Mother a reason for living, "any time spent away from the Mother was wasted time, empty time, dead time . . . in the Mother's company he and everything else came alive." (108) Ignorant of real suffering and real joy he oscillates between a false kind of happiness and false kind of unhappiness. Real suffering begets happiness as Beneett says, "The two are the twins, inseparable from each other." (11) Matteo's escape into the Mother's Ashram becomes a pretext to renounce his worldly duties as a husband and father. Spiritual life does not mean renunciation of worldly duties. Matteo is totally overpowered by what the Mother speaks or suggests. Matteo seeks the Mother's advice with regard to the conflict in his mind and at home, "Tell me what to do, Mother. Living as I do, as a householder with a family, can I continue to live here amongst Sadhus?" (138) Matteo is so deeply absorbed in the work of the press and publication of the master's work that there is little or no time left for family life. Sophie questions him, "Why is the ordinary not enough for you? Home, family, a child?" (141) In order to understand the unknown, Matteo keeps shuttling between his family and the Abode of Bliss. Sophie misunderstands Matteo's love and devotion for the Mother. He clarifies her doubts by saying, there is a difference between sacred and profane love. "Listen in her presence I feel I am more alive. . . . Her presence heightens and illuminates the experience of living as no one else's does . . . when I leave her, I feel I am falling, down into darkness." (141)

J.G. Bennet believes that "Love means to love all. It means to be able to put oneself, to feel oneself in the place of all that exists. It is to share the joys and sufferings of all life." (11) But Matteo's love is not based on this philosophy—it is not all comprehensive. He is totally illusioned and lacks psychological equilibrium. Such a fragmented personality is the outcome of a clash between an individual's attempt to adjust to some situation and his constitutional inability to meet the challenge. Matteo's psychological attributes, social pressures and expectations from self and society place him in unique circumstances to fight against for which he finds himself ill equipped. He feels as if his self-worth is under attack and consequently faces a threat to his existence. He calls Sophie a destroyer. "You are trying to destroy me by destroying the only part that has any value." (142) According to Erich Fromm, "Man's existential contradiction results in a state of constant disequilibrium." Matteo does not follow the abiding values in social life and this inability on his part results in personality disintegration and ontological insecurity. Sorakin observes: "The experiences of these characters lead to the destruction of the network of socio-cultural relationships, resulting in the demoralization of the individual or an increase in his psycho-social isolation."[8]

Matteo's strategy of projection, his tendency to blame Sophie does not help him in coping with the stress and conflict that overwhelms from all sides. He knows he has no strength to stand on his feet. His need of a Guru or a Mother makes him lose his mental strength and confidence to face the world. Matteo adopts a restricted way of living. Owing to long continued suffering and frustration he loses hope. Sophie's comments about the Mother hurt him emotionally. He insults himself to such an extent that he fails to achieve a close affectional relationship again with Sophie. He clarifies to Sophie "I have given myself to her. Why do you want to keep me, Sophie, from pursuing my beliefs?" (160) When the Mother dies, Matteo's journey of transformation is stalled in between. His search for spirituality is unfulfilled and the quest for unity with the supreme and the divine remains unrealized. His anguish and frustration is manifold because while relentlessly following the trail of the divine, he has neglected his duties and responsibilites towards family, society and his own self. Matteo's life according to the Indian thought is not rightly lived and does not achieve a graded ascent. According to the Upanishads, the key to cosmic consciousness is in the consciousness of the soul. Matteo's renunciation leads only to blank emptiness of negation. His ignorance, his limiting of consciousness in the form of the moral image of the Mother, alienating himself from his surroundings, hamper his growth, his free thinking. He is not awake to the highest reality that surrounds him, therefore, he knows not the reality of his own soul. His failures have by no means been trifling, they have strewn his path with colossal ruins, his sufferings have been immense. Lonely, anxious, depressed and dependent, he is fully aware of the mess he is in and is oppressed with the sadness of living till the end of his journey on this planet.

Thus, while depicting the conflict-ridden existence of Matteo, Anita Desai is dealing with the predicament of the modern man caught in the contrived dialectical opposition between 'what is' and 'what ought to be.' The journey to Ithaca is a voyage undertaken to discover the natural wholeness of being and how to experience it in one's day-to-day existence. It attempts to explain why man exists in perpetual conflict, what are the sources of fragmentation and what is the mode of recovering the integrated being. The poem quoted by the novelist in the beginning of the novel hints at the essence of the philosophy in the novel:

> Visit hosts of Egyptian cities. . .
> to learn and learn from those who have knowledge. . .
> rich with all you have gained on the way. . .
> With such great wisdom you have gained,
> With so much experience. . . . (ix)

Retrieval of integration or wholeness or bliss is the outcome of experience, meditation and selfless love. It is a state which comes into being spontaneously, when in total attention, man has clearly understood that nature of the ceaseless process of self-construction. It is a state of total love, freedom and understanding.

NOTES

1. J.P. Sartre, *Being and Nothingness* (New York: Citadel Press, 1966), p. 163.
2. Oswald Spengler, *The Decline of the West* (New York: Alfred A. Knopf, 1947), p. 217.
3. Anita Desai, *Journey to Ithaca* (London: Heinemann, 1995), pp. 18-19.
4. Sri Aurobindo, "Superamental Manifestation," *SABCL,* Vol. 16 (Pondicherry: Sri Aurobindo Ashram, 1971), p. 197.
5. John Macquarrie, *Existentialism* (New York: Pelican, 1972), p. 79.
6. J.C. Coleman, *Abnormal Psychology and Modern Life* (Bombay: D.B. Taraporewala, 1970), p. 97.
7. J.G. Bennet, *The Way to be Free* (New York: Samuel Weiser, 1980), p. 303.
8. P.A. Sorakin, *Social and Cultural Dynamics* (New York, 1937), Vol. III, p. 500.

The Persistence of Memory and History: A Study of Indira Ganesan's *The Journey*

LATHA RENGACHARI and E. MANICKAM

Indira Ganesan's first novel *The Journey* is an interesting source for the study of history and memory as essential parts of most post-colonial expatriate fiction. The motif of travel is central to the text, and the landscape of memory often becomes more significant than reality.

The story abounds with journeys, past and present, which serve to off-set the emotional journey of the protagonist Renu, from superstitious and neurotic fears, towards an awareness of the present and its potentialities. Renu and her parents leave the Island of Pi, for America, when she is a child. She grows into adolescence and adulthood in the west, while keeping memories of childhood exxperiences at Pi, alive in her mind. Her cousin Rajesh dies in a train accident while journeying from Madhupur to Chombatore. The Krishnans—Renu, her mother and sister—return to Pi for the funeral. The novel journeys back in time and memory to the travels of Renu's uncle Adda Krishnamurthy in Europe, in search of a solution against imperialism and an understanding of all imperialistic enterprise. Adda returns ten years later to Pi with a Spanish wife, Alphonsa. Alphonsa's journey to Pi from Europe, and her life in an inhospitable atmosphere amidst Adda's unsympathetic family, is a telling picture of exilic trauma. In the present, Freddie, the itinerant American, journeys across the world from New York to India to find something to give shape to existence. Kish, the adopted son of Amir, the extremist freedom fighter of Pi, embarks on a journey to find hair growth oil. The journey motif continues with the young people—Renu and her friends—setting out on a journey across the island. The novel ends with Renu waiting to set out on her final journey to America, and to freedom. Every one of these journeys in the novels describes exilic experiences of one form or the other. The journey itself, and the trauma attendant on finding oneself in a strange atmosphere, touch the travellers in more ways than one. They are changed people at the end of the journey, changed irrevocably—emotionally and mentally. Every journey is a quest, most often unrewarding as regards the prime motive of the journey, but nonetheless enlightening and enriching for the characters. Each journey is a painful experience, filled with a sense of loneliness, alienation and fear of rejection.

These exilic experiences form the overpowering backdrop that echoes in Renu's memory. Michael Bucknor tallks of memory, in the writing of the South Asian diaspora: "The landscape of memory becomes a site of ambivalence which characterises the experience of South Asians in the diaspora. While the South Asian hankers for the past, memory will reveal that an idealization of that past is difficult since it is embedded in uprootings, tragedy and pain. Post-colonial projects that revisit history in an attempt to present alternative vision of past events ought to be wary of romanticising that past."[1]

The novel suggests that history is determined to a large extent by recollections. Memory, often filtered, fragmemtary, shifting, incomplete and subjective is one determinant of history. The story of the Krishnans and their family, and the lives of the Krishnans in the West, unfolds primarily through recollection. The near past of Renu's childhood and the past of her mother's childhood with her siblings are enacted in Renu's memory. Private events in these lives take place alongside the public events of colonialism/imperialism and the fight for freedom in the subcontinent. The story is not linear, but travels back and forth in time and space. Images of Renu's troubled adolescence, caught between rigid eastern social codes of conduct and the liberal pleasure of the surrounding western tradition intersperse with scenes from Adda Krishnamurthy's experiences in Europe and with Amir's subversive exploits against colonial rule.

All the journeys of the novel from a fine mesh of history—past and present—which throws into relief the journey of Renu into maturity, into an understanding of the present. The discordant discontinuity of the story is reflective of the turmoil in Renu's mind. The past and present interweave to define Renu's future, a future that is freed of the burdens of memory. Vassanji writes of the importance of preserving a sense of one's past through reconstructions of the kind that Renu does: "This need to recreate, mythify, and explain can be traced to two not unrelated factors: The rapid disappearance of a way of life . . . ; and the rapid and continuing modernization of the Third World. Whether the writer stays in his homeland or emigrates, his life has been renewed, and he attempts to understand the past, and from it the present."[2] The importance of this preservation makes it a communal act involving different individuals and incorporating several generations. The community on Pi contributes to the preservation of the myths and memories. The family itself, the grandfather and many aunts and other relatives, contribute to the keeping alive of the past. The recording of all these memories, however disjointed, is the writer's attempt at "fixing" a fleeting way of life. Memory has other functions too. The past is recorded so that the future becomes more understandable. The novel does not remain in the past. Ganesan does not glamorise the past and remain bound to nostalgia, ruminating on what was. The journey backward, to Renu/Ganesan is a compulsory journey so as to gain an understanding of the future. Renu's near neurotic fantasies are the result of the conflict between adolescent fears and uncomfortable notions of duty towards a tradition that she is not sure of, a tradition that abounds in superstition and myth, catalysed by the death of her cousin and the attendant rituals. Caught between two traditions, Renu has trouble balancing her American upbringing and its inherent western rationality with the inherited traditions of her Island ancestors and the need to conform to the expectations of her maternal family. She constantly ruminates on the great differences between her lifestyle in New York and that on the island. This causes her confused mind more trauma. She thinks:

> So much was different on Pi. Here no gesture was private, the sweep of the family buffered all movement, all thoughts. Everything was discussed except family secrets. It had been another thing in New York. Renu's parents were scientists and their lives were austere, defined, tangible. One lived, one ate, one read newspapers and rarely trusted anyone. "You were born in the space age," their father would say, and Renu and Manx grew up believing they could become astronauts. Except for a shelf of ivories and bronzes depicting dancing gods, there was no trace of Pi in their house on Long Island. . . . The house changed, though, with their father's death. The Americanization and westernization with which he'd tried so hard to shape their lives began to fall away. Aerogrammes from Pi reintroduced myth into their lives, stories he'd banished. From the aunts came good-day charts and advice. . . . Rukmani put away her coordinated pantsuits and wore saris from Lexington Avenue under her lab coats. She curtailed the girls' activities, refusing to allow them dances and late nights.[3]

The novel abounds with details about the differences in the two ways of life that Renu experiences. She looks back to the time of their arrival at New York and is amazed at her parents' capacity for adaptation and at how her mother weathered the transition, a symbol of grit and determination. She talks of the trauma of having to live like a typical island girl amidst her American school friends, always having to invent excuses for not participating in peer group activities because of her mother's strictures. Renu is more traumatized by myth and memory and is more confused by the differences in the two cultures betwixt which she is caught, than her sister Manx, to whom reality is the American existence that she knows. Totally caught up in the present moment, Manx sees life on Pi as a change of circumstances, offering her variety in her young life.

Renu's journey down memory is essential. Her fears and the resultant illness are the direct result of the conflict that she feels, caught as she is, like other Third World expatriates in the west, between two contrasting ways of life. She, like other members of the South Asian diaspora, feels a certain responsibility towards her traditional past, to her roots—a responsibility which is in conflict with the liberal western tradition of her present life. Blithely ignoring the traditions of the island is impossible for Renu and doing so would cause guilt feelings. The journey into the collective memory of the island and her own personal memory serves to put the past in perspective, and to redefine her own existence in the present. She realizes that there are no absolutes in life, no givens as to the path she had to take. She understands that she has to create an absolute for herself. In a telling conversation, she asks Freddie if the books that he reads give him guidance. He replies:

> Not so much guidance as a presentation of a variety of thought. I mean, we all have this *choice* before us, different ways of perception. I was thinking, it's different from, say, math, where you operate from a base of givens, of absolutes. From the absolutes, you can prove a theorem about a triangle, but only if you have a given. In our lives, we have no givens, really, and end up groping, trying to stumble upon a truth without knowing the path to follow. If we had a given, it'd be much easier.
>
> Life and death are givens.
>
> Right. Life and death and birth and rebirth—it's a cycle, and we can never be sure of where we are exactly. . . .
>
> Do you think that even if we don't know the absolutes, that they still exist?
>
> Depends if you believe in a God or not. I mean, we can create absolutes, like a religion, or a type of diet. . . . At some point, we all have to create an absolute. (168)

Renu decides to go back to America, to enter college there. She understands that the past is important but resolves not to let it hold her in thrall. She acknowledges the traditions of her island past but refuses to let it hold her back from the present and its promises. The west and the life that it offers become her absolutes and she steps "away from her inherited weights, demanding flight," and "a mobility that can hold the keys of the universe."

The recording of the past in the novel is important as Ganesan insists on the confrontation of the past by the expatriate in order to take the step into the future. The presentation of history and memory is not romanticised—the past is stated in a rather prosaic manner—the voices of rationality, those of Adda and Manx, interspersing with the mythology expounded by Renu's aunts. Renu's emphatic escape from the grasp of superstitions and myths is almost clinically described:

> Renu made another list:
> 1. They killed the monkey with the arrow.
> 2. The monkey was divine and chose to be shot.
> 3. The arrow's flight and the monkey's fall had nothing to do with one another.
> She stared at the paper as if she'd written her own destiny. (168)

The incident of the monkey's accidental death while she and her cousin Rajesh had been playing with arrows as children, traumatises her all through life, and is symbolic of her total preoccupation with myth. With the writing down of this list, she does indeed write her own destiny as it indicates that she has put the past and its attendant fears, firmly behind her. Ganesan/Renu refuses to remain in the past, idyllic or traumatic. The present and its pleasures and pains are the only realities for her. The novel refuses to be seen as literature of nostalgia or as an ode to a glamorised past tradition, as much Third World literature is. The novel is an acknowledgement, by the expatriate writer in the west, of the necessity for remembering, however painful it is, in order to come to terms with the present.

NOTES

1. "Mudbound in Memory: Shifting Sand or Solid Rock?—Postcolonial Enquiries in M.G. Vassanji's *The Gunny Sack," Toronto Review of Contemporary Writing Abroad*, 14.1, Summer 1995, pp. 15-27.
2. Qtd. in Bucknor.
3. Indira Ganesan, *The Journey* (New York: Alfred A. Knopf, 1990), p. 21.

Vikram Seth's *The Golden Gate*: Some First Impressions

RAGINI RAMACHANDRA

If the publication of *The Golden Gate* made an immediate sensation in 1986 as "*tour de force,*" *A Suitable Boy* made "publishing history" in 1993 (so we are told by the doting media *ad nauseum*) not only attracting unprecedented attention from all quarters but making its author, the blue-eyed boy of recent Indian fiction in English and even placing him in the race for the highest honour, the Nobel Prize! All the national newspapers have vied with one another to mark him out as 'a writer with the golden pen,' 'a writer with a golden touch,' 'a possible genius' and so on and so forth. A plethora of articles hailing Vikram Seth and his work in superlative terms makes one wonder whether critics have not gone all out to disprove Seth himself about the possible success of his first work, *The Golden Gate*:

> Professor, publisher, and critic
> Each voiced his doubts. I felt misplaced.
> A writer is a mere arthritic
> Among these muscular Gods of taste.
> As for that sad blanemange, a poet
> The world is hard; he ought to know it.
> Driveling in rhyme's all very well;
> The question is, does spittle sell? (5.2)

The point is that his 'spittle' has sold (and it will sell as long as there is an uncritical audience to lap it up) and as best seller too, assigning him to the category of those fortunates who have greatness *thrust* upon them. The passage just quoted while betraying poor taste leaves one in no doubt about the author's nonchalance towards his vocation and his readers. If the tone here is bantering and irreverential, elsewhere it is, to say the least, contemptuous and derogatory as when he looks upon the 'muscular Gods of taste' as 'Worms,' as boring worms which feed on a writer's corpse. But in the presence of all the praise and encomium lavished upon him now, Seth himself must be in for a pleasant surprise or does he take it as his rightful due?

Yet when all this din and glamour has relatively died down, it is for the serious and discerning student/ scholar/ teacher to ask himself where exactly the success lies and whether the celebrity status accorded to Seth is at all warranted.

I shall concentrate on *The Golden Gate* since it was this novel with its unusual form that first catapulted Seth to fame. Reading through the pages of the novel for the first time, I was often reminded of the scene where Polonius asks Prince Hamlet: 'What do you read, my lord?' and Prince Hamlet replies with seething sarcasm, 'Words, Words, Words.' That is what *The Golden Gate* is, whether at first or subsequent readings, not so much a masterpiece of designing as an amazing display of mental gymnastics! (*Chamatkāra*) The reader who has to wade through much verbiage is literally swamped and caught in an avalanche of words. Even for one who treasures all forms of artistic expression, the book is a melange of words which comes perilously close to making Seth's own remarks about his characters in the course of the novel *real*:

> Engulfed in . . . *cerebral clatter,*
> John writhes. . . (3.32, italics mine)

and

> Ed spouts forth a distracting babble
> of *witty entertaining trash*. (4.22, italics mine)

"Cerebral clatter" and "witty entertaining trash" aptly seem to articulate the reader's own initially unformulated opinion.

An obsession with words perhaps accounts for the generous sprinkling of strange and obscure vocabulary, tongue twisting names and a rhyme scheme that degenerates into cheap gimmicks on certain occasions. What is one to make of words like:

> Picosecond, pleonastic, fescne, catholicon,
> goop, anaconda, tumescence, luculent,
> flotsam, fortissimo, glob, chardonnay,
> maculate, sozzled, stogie, imprimatur

to quote only a few random selections.

And as for rhyme scheme, once again a few samples might be examined:

> As if to prove that all is flux,
> Your squalid cat pissed on my tux.
> . . . Cats and iguana
> Lie sunk in somnolent Nirvana . . .
> they on the bread pile cheese, lettuce and salami
> Enough to satisfy an army
> . . . sheds a tear
> That she won't see her for a year
> . . . man and wife
> set sail on the calm pond of life. . . .
> He sees with vision like a knife
> Into the very heart of life.

'Datatronics' must rhyme with 'histrionics'; 'iguana' with 'Ecbatana'; 'stuffy with scruffy'; 'ways' with 'haze' and this goes on until it smacks of being undergraduatish. But interestingly, Seth is supposed to have told an interviewer:

> rhyme and metre are perversely liberating. If you aren't entirely bound by the "cat/mat" kind of rhyme but have worked with rhyme for a number of years, you find that, just as certain dance forms could hardly be called constraining because they are stylized in some sense but in fact can be more expressive than a looser movement might be, so rhyme and metre, if used effectively, can be enhancing features. They can make many a funny passage funnier and a sad passage sadder.

While such a device could at times be entertaining, it cannot be overlooked that a surfeit of it could be counter-productive creating just the opposite effect. Even where the rhyme scheme is not obtrusive, the very medium of a novel like this, which is verse runs the risk of hogging all the attention to *itself*, and the genre itself is the chief novelty about this book, its forte, its chief claim to distinction according to critics. But the moot point is whether the medium itself could be the message and whether that could in itself constitute a criterion for greatness. While one admits that this radical departure from convention could be considered an achievement of sorts, one must hasten to add that it is both the strength and the weakness of the novel, for while the medium has earned the novel its much-vaunted publicity it has also trapped its word-drunk author in its strangle-hold, often forcing him to resort to mere tricks of style and manipulation of language. Besides, one is not sure of the justification of using high-sounding verse to describe the trivial and the mundane especially when it is unredeemed making the dichotomy between the ludicrousness of the subject and the loftiness of its treatment glaring. In the face of so much verse being expended for instance upon the three pet cats in the novel, Charlmagne in particular, one is compelled to note that apart from producing some amusing moments, and the microscopically detailed accounts notwithstanding, here, the cat is a cat is a cat, as against the splendid use it is put to in Raja Rao's *Cat and Shakespeare.*

As for style, it is somewhat comical that this modish writer should revert to the Victorian practice of addressing the Reader now and then as 'Gentle Reader,' 'Dear Reader' etc! The butting in of the authorial voice tends to be quite an unwelcome intrusion.

Besides, there is nothing in the book to suggest his *Indian* identity except perhaps three words, 'circa,' 'Nirvana' and 'Buddha' scattered across its pages.

The foregoing analysis perhaps gives the impression that craftsmanship is Vikram Seth's alter ego and not without reason. This juggler of words might have displayed mercurial talent and wit, might even have managed his verse at places with consummate skill, but is this a body of verse that can *stand*, one wonders. And what are his concerns and preoccupations, his perceptions and his insights, one might very well ask, which takes us to the very theme of the novel.

The setting is San Francisco, the city of Saint Francis, 'the loveliest city in the world'—'light pearled,' 'fog-fingered,' 'pinnacled' with its famous bay—the 'unruffled daughter of the pacific' glimmering in the evening with light from the golden globes of its street lamps—'like sequins on black velvet robes.' Apart from these few vivid touches and memorable descriptions the city itself hardly comes to life as Françe or England does at Raja Rao's hands. But the milieu and ethos of life lived there, of yuppies and urban officials, of artists and ordinary people gets successfully evoked.

The novel is basically the story of a man who cannot get love in life and ends up much the same way as he begins—a lonely human being. When the novel opens, we realize that John's mother is dead and he is "caught in the kelp of loneliness." One cannot miss the parallel with Rama of *The Serpent and the Rope*. Born an orphan he remains one wandering round the world, sobbing for his mother; his restless search assuming in the process the status of a quest. To a sensitive reader, John's predicament too might carry intimations of a metaphysical problem; of basic human condition; of man's orphaned existence on earth.

The novel ranges through all the important facets of human life: love, marriage, birth, death. An exploration of these vital issues brings to the fore some problems still by and large peculiar to affluent societies of the west, the American in particular, such as unhappy marriages, broken homes, single parenthood, divorce and homosexuality.

John, the protagonist of the novel who lost his mother young used to chafe even as a small boy against the fate that had been meted out to him. Robbed of a mother's love; devoid of a family to 'cushion his solitude'; no spouse, no sibling, no children; he is advised by his former love Janet Hayakawa who still maintains friendly relations with him to insert matrimonial ads in the papers. The responses it evokes from various women, the events that follow thereafter provide some hilarious moments in the novel not to speak of wit and irony. After interviewing a couple of women, John settles for Elisabeth Dorati, 'Sweet Liz,' she too a little lonely except for her infamous cat Charlmagne. With her golden hair and vibrant verve, she charms John who in his elation can't figure out whether she is a woman or 'divine illusion'!

The loving pair are enveloped in an 'amorous mist' for a time, their heads surrounded by a halo of rosy light. John, a loner has at last found a new home, and someone to love in 'life's brief game.' He and Liz co-habit for a while enjoying the bliss of togetherness until the storm blows that brings home the truth that 'all life's a shaky dream.' All the quirks that delighted John first later aggrieves him. He can't get over the feeling that Liz loves the cat more than him! Constant friction between the two on account of the cat and Liz's sudden decision to marry Phil, John's school chum, who happens to be not merely a divorcee and the father of a six-year-old boy, but a bi-sexual, having had physical relations with Ed, Liz's own brother, drives John to an 'embittered brooding/ against the cosmos.' Pain 'mangles' John who believes he is 'duped' by love. 'So all her talk of love was spurious,' he bemoans. Hurt by Liz and Phil's 'breach of trust' he spurns all their attempts at reconciliation. 'Lonely and injured in his pride/ His sorrow festers.' He is lost in savage transportation of grievance. Then leads a life of dissipation, 'sifting bars each night/ For cute chicks.' Then follows a time when he even gets 'resigned/ To loneliness.' But Liz herself, torn between conflicting emotions and to loyalties is somewhat like the poor little bird which keeps yearning between her winter and summer home in A.D. Hope's "Death of a Bird." It is when John's friendships have all gone astray that he thinks of his former love, Janet Hayakawa whom he has treated 'less than ideally.' Jan who at one time was 'mad' about him and 'could hardly think of life without him' responds to his friendly gestures and applies a healing touch. With her voice she even restores him to 'gentleness.'

The two slowly slip back to their old days of 'fire and smoke.' Now a 'quilt of peace' surrounds John, he dreams of nothing and is even 'free of all volition.' It astounds him to think how little the enmity of the crass world, its fickle illness can now impinge on his 'crypt of stillness.' And so the days pass. Intent upon patching up differences between erstwhile friends John and Liz and Phil, Janet invites the latter home to a party. But as destiny would have it, even as the guests are arriving for the night's revels, news of Jan's involvement in a car accident reaches John leaving him utterly dazed. Jan succumbs to her injuries in a hospital where John, not being next of kin cannot even be allowed inside to see her just as life is ebbing out of her body. In his intense despair he broods that, had he managed to say a word to her she might have survived. Jan's friends, the Lammonts too die in the crash leaving their little son the sole surviour of the accident. Both the sorrow of an orphan and the anguish of a bereaved lover are movingly portrayed and it is in the handling of this crisis that the novel suddenly acquires a depth and a dimension hitherto unsuspected.

John who is completely shattered by this unexpected disaster becomes a nervous wreck. Haunted by images of Jan, her face, her eyes, her voice, it looks he can't outlive this pain. The reader grieves for him as 'he tries to wring/ Meaning from things that have no meaning/ And scrapes at rusted words that yield/ few glints of insight.' (13.26) In his grief John can attain a stature, a state of mind where he indulges through briefly in meditations of a philosophical nature which have an echo of Hamlet's ruminations and even allows himself to an expression of 'prayer' so as to find a pattern in or cure for Jan's death. But life must go on and so Liz requests him to play the godfather to her new-born son whom she has chosen to call John.

The novel ends with John poignantly hearing Jan's voice saying to him 'I'm with you, John. You are not alone' thus bringing John's explorative voyage, if it can be called one, to an end. The wheel has come full circle. 'What did not last in life has now possessed John wholly.' It looks as if the invisible bridge is the only kind of bridge man is destined to build . . . to reach out . . . to reach across . . . to people and not any concrete one that the city of San Francisco boasts of.

Thus the last section which compensates for the earlier frivolity proves to be the novel's sole redemption. Thematically, the novel *has* the potentialities of serious fiction, but the extremely quizzical mode of handling the material except in the last part is, what one fears, has reduced the book to the category of predominantly an entertainer.

Towards Affirmation: A Reading of Arun Joshi's "A Trip for Mr. Lele" and "Survivor"

E. SATYANARAYANA

With five novels and a collection of short stories to his credit, Arun Joshi is regarded as one of the important contemporary fiction writers. He was catapulted to literary fame when his novel *The Last Labyrinth* earned him the much-coveted Sahitya Akademi Award for the year 1982. Undoubtedly, his untimely demise in 1993 is a big blow to the field of Indian writing in English.

Much of the criticism on his creative output, both novels and short stories, claims that Arun Joshi is an existentialist novelist writing in line with Albert Camus and Franz Kafka. As a matter of fact, with his advent on the Indian literary scene, the fiction in English has shifted its focus from social realism to psychological realism. He has attempted to explore the depths of the psyche of an individual trapped in the matrix of decaying human values. The characters in his fiction seem to have been engaged in a relentless search for true being.

Besides, Arun Joshi in his fiction, displays an awareness of what makes for human tragedy in the society. He sees that the forces of industrialization and urbanization have exerted a deleterious influence on the life of man. Consequently, even the relationship between husband and wife is reduced to the condition of a commodity essentially. It is this aspect of life which in Arun Joshi's view has marred the human essence as could be found not only in his novels but also in his short fiction. This aspect has largely suffered a neglect at the hands of the critics.

Except for a few passing references, not much effort is made to evaluate Arun Joshi's short fiction which touches on the varied issues that predetermine the existence of man. The present paper seeks to examine the thematic concerns of Arun Joshi with reference to the stories "A Trip for Mr. Lele" and "Survivor." These stories, along with eight others, appeared in 1975 under the title *Survivor*[1] which, as C.V. Venugopal rightly observes, is a collection of "artistically satisfying pieces" and Joshi here "probes the alienated individual with sympathy and understanding."[2]

The protagonists in both the stories are hapless husbands and sensitive fathers whose separation from their daughters helps them emerge from their cocoon-like existence and rebel to realize their personal freedom.

"A Trip for Mr. Lele" is a touching tale of a sentimental relationship between a conscientious father and a disabled daughter. Mr. Lele, the central figure, is the highest paid vendor of toothpastes in the country, next only to his boss to whom he is accountable. However, the job is not a bed of roses because he has to always maintain the rise in the sale by employing innovative gift schemes. So he carries on with his job, in spite of himself. He often thinks of resigning and stamping on the "horn-rimmed glasses" of his boss who being practical, does not care for sentiments and tries to extract more from him. Mr. Lele is helpless. Besides, he is a victim of the subversive ideals of his wife, Mrs. Lele. Interestingly, it is she who keeps him back, unlike other women, not by tears or threats but by simly letting him know of her social status. She is a representative of the "western emancipation and oriental indolence." (72) She believes that marriage is a "solemn contract" and it is the duty of man to "provide for the five meals, the insurance, the weekly party, the children's fees, the electricity bills, the telephone bills, the medical bills, the annual vacation, a change of saries, occasional jewellery . . . perfume and a job for the wife's brother." (72) It is her personality and the force of her ideas that have obliged Mr. Lele to believe that the contract is "not only as solemn as something the violation of which might let loose divine retribution." (73) Over the years he has developed a fatalistic attitude towards life. He makes no attempt to impose his will on his wife. He is obliging in his dealings. But he is a responsible father. He has a daughter who is pale and small for her age. She also has a club foot. He is very much concerned for her. It is not really love but a sense of sympathy that draws him to the handicapped child. He finds in her "all the beautiful and perishable things with which so much of life's mansion is furnished." (73) He longs to be in her company to let her feel assured. He is always careful not to let his official responsibilities interfere with his paternal obligations. He cannot brook to see his daughter suffer anymore since she is already struck with "so disabling and grotesque an affliction." (73) He is filled with a secret sorrow for the pathetic condition of the child. It is this sentimental concern of a father towards his daughter which gives the story a human touch.

The physical deformity of the child symbolically represents Mr. Lele's own inability to articulate his inner protest against both his wife and his boss before whom he appears as weak and fragile as the child. It is perhaps the realization of his weakness which makes him more attached to the child than to his wife. To compensate, as it were, for the terrible injustice meted out to the child by fate, Mr. Lele makes it a habit of keeping her happy while his wife is busy attending to the problems of Ladies' club. He takes pleasure in satisfying every wish of hers. In fact, he finds a sense of solace in her presence. The important thing that he never missess is her birthday which is only five days away when the story begins.

About this time, Mr. Lele is compelled to leave for Bombay and then to Hyderabad to save the falling trade. Having promised to return on her birthday, he reluctantly goes on the trip. But it takes more time than he expects and he feels anxious about the child back home. He sends a telegram saying that he may not attend her birthday. Symbolically, the trip Mr. Lele undertakes from north to south brings about a transformation in him. His sojourn in different places and his confrontation with different situations peel the layers off his self which he for the first time finds in his own way and rebels.

In fact, his heart lies in his daughter. The farther he travels, the nearer he feels to the child mentally. He fails to show any interest either in his assignment or in the new places which sans his daughter appear dull and drab. His nausea increases. He simply stops speaking. But can he rebel out and out? Ironically, he is aware of his own limitations. He has to think of "his contract with his wife, his firm, with the forces of circumstances." (77) However, the inevitable has to take place. On his final trip, he confronts a boy who has the makings of an artist. The boy tells Mr. Lele that he wants to paint "the sea, the sky, the sun, the stars, the night, especially the night, and even the wind, except that . . . has no colour." (81) He says further that he had a sister whom he loved dearly. But when she died of leukemia, he was not informed as he was away at school. This sad tale of the boy really touches Mr. Lele and he, thinking only of his daughter, takes the next flight to Delhi to greet her on her birthday and it costs him his job.

The story "Survivor" assumes significance in that it reflects Arun Joshi's basic concern in the anthology. It focuses not only on the growing dominance of modern women in all spheres of life but on the resultant rupture in the human relationships both in the family and the society, on account of urbanization and commercialization.

Kewal Kappor, the narrator-protagonist of "Survivior" is a typical modern man who has no illusions about the progress made by human civilization. Like Mr. Lele he also suffers at the hands of his indifferent wife. But he is more eloquent in his expression of protest than his counterpart. However they serve as foils to each other. Relegated to the position of "an engine for manufacturing money," (33) he feels isolated.

Arun Joshi effectively employs the device of dramatic monologue to reveal the inner self of the protogonist who, unable to adapt to the prevailing social norms, "sets sail towards terrible shipwrecks." (90) He provides us an insight into the life of middle class people who, in this anxiety to reach the higher rungs of the social ladder, hurtle down to the pits of eternal despair and lose the essence of their beings.

What Kewal Kapoor wants is a "bit of love, a pinch of that good old love that demure little Hindu wives are exuding . . . in epics and stuff" (83) and a constant talk of money. Kapoor dislikes everything, particularly all that associated with money. But as an ideal husband, he is expected to earn to meet the growing needs of his wife. He leaves one job for another till he gets fixed up in a drugs company where he has to do with the public relations. Ironically, he himself has many a complaint to voice, but he is fated to listen to the complaints of others. Though he tries to do his best in his new assignment, it takes him no time to realize that he is a misfit. Denied a change of job, he is overwhelmed with a sense of boredom and he becomes an introvert. He forgets how to laugh. The agony of not belonging is so intense in him that he runs away from his office so as to find peace of mind in the artificial things like cinema and transistor radio. As a result, he gets hooked up to the Indian theatres seeing twenty films a month. He admits:

> that was a turning point . . . only time I wasn't cracking up was when I was wallowing in the goddammed make-believe and listening to the mushy songs. (85)

His infatuation with self-fulfilment through films, sometimes flirting with girls results in the loss of his job. He is estranged from his wife. However, it does not scare him. He moves from one place to another only to feel despair and depressed. He realizes that the modern society with all its progress is devoid of human love and sympathy and money is the be all and end all of life. Fed up with "money talking imbecile world," Kapoor inches towards total alienation from the society. Interestingly, it is the thought of his daughter that brings him back and gives a sense of relief to his tormented soul.

The only two persons who love him in the world are his brother, Robu and his little daughter. He confesses: "I kept missing my daughter. As Divali drew closer I grew desperate. I just had to see her. I was terrified she would forget me." (93-94) Thus, obsessed with an urge to see her, he joins hands with thieves who putting on masks, enter the house on the day of Diváli. While he enjoys the company of his child, his associates rob people of jewellery. Ridiculous it may seem though, the act of Kewal Kapoor has a sense of inevitability about it to assert his right to love. It also suggests that it is only love that sustains human relations and imparts meaning to human existence.

The story of Kewal Kapoor recalls the problem of Billy Biswas of Joshi's *The Strange Case of Billy Biswas*. Billy is disillusioned with the phoney values of the modern world and he leaves for the primitive world. He becomes one with the tribals who are free from the hypocrisy of the mainstream urban life. Similarly, Kapoor also leaves his home. But unlike Billy, Kapoor attempts to realize his individuality and consolidate his position in the society not away from it. Kapoor is not as idealistic as Billy. However, he, like Billy, is in quest for a humane society which is filled with natural love and where people feel secure in one another's company.

In the end, Kewal Kapoor, after throwing the booty into the dark sea, utters a few words which indict the dehumanized morals of the modern society. He is scathing in his outburst: "I am a survivor of that fantastic racket that passes for the MODERN INDIAN SOCIETY . . . of that greatest disaster of them all: THE MODERN INDIAN WOMAN." (96)

The protogonists of both stories—"A Trip for Mr. Lele" and "Survivor"—are placed in a similar predicament. They are survivors of the cataclysms and disasters of the so-called progressive society. Being alive to their inner self, they defy the system which tries to encroach on their personal freedom. Mr. Lele and Kapoor crave for simple love which they find in their daughters who as innocent children serve as invisible bonds between the over-riding mothers and sensitive fathers. The society which traps and challenges man, also provides a way for liberation. And it is man who has to fight to realize his dream of freedom. As such, a transformation from conformity to confrontation is discernible in the two narratives.

NOTES

1. Arun Joshi, *Survivor* (New Delhi: Sterling, 1975)
2. C.V. Venugopal, "The Indian English Short Story" *Perspectives on Indian Fiction in English*, ed. M.K. Naik (New Delhi: Abhinav, 1985), p. 231.

Arun Joshi's *The Apprentice*: The Novel of Our Times

C. N. SRINATH

Nearly fifteen years ago, sometime after the publication of Arun Joshi's *The Apprentice* I had discussed it as one of the few novels of great distinction to have come out of India after the work of the three major novelists, R.K. Narayan, M.R. Anand and Raja Rao. On going back to it, after this considerable interval I find the novel has retained its pointed relevance for us in India, or for that matter for any one in the contemporary world steeped in corruption of all kinds. This only speaks for the merit of the novel in not being passe and in preserving its freshness and urgency in the tone of communication. It is also true things have not changed in India for the novel to be irrelevant. But *The Apprentice* has an intrinsic artistic relevance which is not totally dependent on the socio-political scene it portrays. It is this that compels the reader to go back to this sad, haunting tale of not only Ratan Rathor, the protagonist-narrator, but of the listener as well. That Mr. Joshi has created a novel without a well-defined plot or characters but just out of the rambling talk of the narrator on a theme which has become stale like yesterday's newspaper is a tribute to his art.

The Apprentice (1974) is an appropriate title which describes its protagonist Ratan Rathor who starts life as an apprentice with all the innocence at his reserve but gradually gets oiled by the machinery of the officialdom that enables him to snake his way up the ladder of success and build up a career. He is hard-working, efficient, patriotic, self-righteous, has a sense of idealism in recalling the incident of his father walking with his chest up to the British gun that mows him down; he is fired by Subhas Bose's example, mellowed by Gandhiji's *sadhana* and sacrifice; he is conscious of his moral superiority but he is a coward, a fake, a sham and the realisation of this is in a search which is so authentic and sincere, in a tone that is introspective and honest to the core that makes it a poignant tale of our times, the post-Independence India. The telling of the tale, in its narrative technique, has some echoes of

Camus's *The Outsider* where the theme of alienation and the existentialist attitude to life lends the style its detachment. But Arun Joshi has made it a truly Indian story with his deep preoccupations and concerns with the Indian earth and its people by analysing himself, in other words, our hypocrisies, our cowardice, our lack of shame, in such a searing way that reminds us of Gandhiji's *My Experiments with Truth*. Corruption at various levels and of different kinds that we notice in society is told with astounding candour that the narrator, who has now lost the capacity to be shocked, thanks to his own experience, asks his imaginary listener: "You are shocked? I suppose the young have a right to be shocked. If there is sawdust in flour and common salt in Penicillin, why my dear friend, why can't men be expected to buy proxies in the hall of death. Anyway, I for one do not have the right to judge."

But it is the use of past tense and the story being told in retrospect that gives the novel its familiar objectivity. It is with such ease he can move deeper and deeper into himself and the vortex of his feeling and thought as he is an apprentice of a different kind, a man without honour but full of profound humility. The way he recalls his earlier days of initiation is astonishing:

> And now that the desks had been cleared for my initiation he gave to me of his craft with open hands. Craft is the wrong word. What he transmitted was a mystique, a style he geared not necessarily to getting things done but of making events obey your will whichever side it happened to be employed upon. The right or the wrong of the side one took was not in question, nor were there touchstones by which one chose. No morals were involved. It was the skill in manoeuvre that mattered which more or less was an end in itself. One was like a sailor on lake, concerned not with a destination but only into the manipulation of the sails, the riding of the wind. (53)

Being a shrewd insight into the ways of officials, the passage maintains an almost metaphysical stance in depicting their amoral operation. It is a deftness that is perilously close to virtuosity but is here saved by the author's sense of the concrete and his eye on situation and character. What might have been a moral fall seems to have been averted by a sense of shame that one notices in the apprentice towards the end. The apprentice shows a remarkable self-awareness in ruthlessly exposing his oversubtleties, fads, preoccupations, self-deceptions, ego and boredom of the dark phase of his life. It is this, along with his present strength to laugh at his meaningless past, that gives a kind of complexity to the character of Ratan. The episode of his article on 'crisis of character' which he now calls a 'comic document' is quite revealing. The whole account is rendered by the narrator with tongue in cheek as we are finally told: "I sent the article to many newspapers but none of them published it. This did not prevent me from having it cyclostyled and distributed among a large number of my friends. I also presented it in the form of a lecture to a couple of Associations in our area." (77)

What one notices here is not hypocrisy, for there is also an element of foolish sincerity, but the lack of drive or moral courage to practice what he preaches. Immediately after this episode we witness his stark statement about his acceptance of a bribe not because of any need but for reasons which are beyond a simple and straight explanation. The whole business of living is so much muddled and has become a whirlpool of confusing values, contradictions and enigmas that he fails to comprehend the meaning of such acts:

> What was right? What was wrong? No one seemed to know. Or, may be they knew, but when it came to practice no one seemed to be sure whether what was right was practicable. That was where the rub lay. And enveloping all this. A fog beyond the fog, were words Like today, words, words, words. Speeches, editorials, resolutions, handouts, slogans, posters, banners, proceedings of the numerous assemblies. It was not the pros and cons of a case that we weighed as we weighed the men behind them. And the men were weighed in money or power it soon became apparent to me that those who had neither were worthless. (48-49)

From the initial restlessness to apathy and even cunning is what we notice in the apprentice. This has led to an inner corrosion of tragic dimension because of the pervasive nature of this epidemic that turns the millions into Nobodies. The contrast between the earlier Ratan, the apprentice who has hitched his wagon to the star of success and Ratan, the apprentice, who has passed through the dark night of the soul, is brought out in the anger, remorse, and intense suffering that one can feel in the tone of the narrative. The character of the Brigadier is presented to highlight in fictional terms, the victimization of the innocent in a corrupt society. As if to focus the enormous and sprawling vitiation of human values the novelist chooses the predicament of the Brigadier who represents the acme of man's sacrifice in his fight for his fellowmen and gives a dramatic turn to the story by making him a victim at the very hands of his closest friend, Ratan who clears the defective war-material. This in turn leaves the Brigadier stunned, and paralyzed having to face a courtmartialling on a charge of desertion on the battlefield. The S.P. who makes a penetrating enquiry exposes Ratan Rathor's grave offence but for lack of proper evidence helplessly pleads with him to confess as a final act of saving his Brigadier friend. Ratan, of course, bravely walks out, mentally resolved to save his friend, but the way he relaxes, dodges and finally writes out his confession, modifies it instantly and tries to justify his act by convincing himself of his 'innocence' and finally pocketing the letter forever shows his efforts to glaze his cowardice with something that passes for martyrdom and innocence by turns. The poor Brigadier, however, cannot wait till his friend makes up his mind and he kills himself. So Ratan Rathor with a deeply troubled conscience goes to Himmat Singh (who has bribed him at the instance of the higher authorities) to avenge his friend's death but soon realizes the absurdity of the whole thing and reflects: "That is a terrible sensation. My friend—may God preserve you from it—the realization that one's life has been a great mistake; without purpose, without results. There are many sorrows of a wasted life. All else, thoughts of revenge, a pleasure, of pain pale before it are made pointless." (194) The apprentice's sense of the futility of it all scalds him inwardly and leaves him so exhausted that he tells his listener most pathetically:

> So you see, my friend, here I am, a man without honour, a man without shame. Perhaps a man of our times. How do I know life has purpose? Actually, I don't. And, quite honestly, mine is not the mind that can grasp such questions. But let me tell you something that a colleague of mine used to say. Life is zero, he would add, you can take nothing away from a zero. . . . I have begun to see a flaw in the argument. You can make it negative. Life might well be a zero, for all I know, but it seems to me that it need not be negative. And it becomes negative when you take out of it your sense of shame, your honour. (204-5)

That Ratan Rathor, who is not an intellectual like Sindi of *The Foreigner* or Billy of *The Strange Case of Billy Biswas* but an ordinary man of ordinary deeds should appreciate the distinction between zero as negative and, implicitly zero as positive speaks for the character's development. And to make it credible the subtle distinction is put in the mouth of a colleague. He is naturally amused now by some of the pet illusions that man nurses and is reminded of the *pujari* (priest) who used to retort, when teased about his profession as chanting mere mumbo-jumbo, doing nobody any good: "He would say: I am here to be of use. And one thing I can do, the only thing that I have been taught to do, is to shout this mumbo-jumbo. And so that is what I do. Not only for myself. For every one. Foolishly, blindly. But what reason is there my friends, he would ask, what reason is there to suppose that the making of money or of a chair, or the pursuit of women is any the less foolish, or less blind?" (203) Hence, out of sorrow and humilation groping to understand the meaning of life and as if to expiate his sin Ratan Rathor undergoes the strangest apprenticeship in the world, namely, wiping the shoes of the congregation sitting on steps outside the temple every morning on his way to the office:

> You do not understand why I do what I do at the temple? It is a little odd, I must admit. A little silly, too. But all apprentices look silly, don't they? A carpenter's assistant, the boy who works the bellows, the novice with the shaven head. Consider me an apprentice and you will perhaps understand. Each morning, before, I go to work, I come here. I sit on the steps of the temple and while they pray, I wipe the shoes of the congregation. Then, when they are gone, I stand in the doorway. I never enter the temple. I am not concerned with what goes on in there. I stand at the doorstep and I fold my hands, my hands smelling of leather and I say things. Be good, I tell myself. Be good. Be decent. Be of use. Then I beg fogiveness of a large, host: my father, my mother, the Brigadier the unknown dead of the war, of those whom I harmed, with deliberation and with cunning, of all those who have been the victims of my cleverness, those I could have helped and did not. After this I get into the car and go to office. And during the day whenever I find myself getting to be clever, lazy, vain, indifferent, I put up my hands to my face and there is the smell of a hundred feet that must at that moment be toiling somewhere and I am put in my place. (206-7)

What *The Apprentice* is not is its distinction—it is neither an existentialist novel, nor is it a confessional story nor a modern novel depicting human angst, not even a success and failure story but an Indian tale which goes to the deeper resources of the tradition to seek more than snap solutions to problems, to involve oneself in an exploration which gives an inner strength in the presence of such contemporary anarchy. The final act of expiation is symbolic, suggestive of profound humility and certainly not another act of the fake out to deceive himself or others. Interestingly, the final scene of Narayan's *The Guide* where Raju is poised to appear as an impresario with seemingly rhetorical declarations is also a success story but it is the subtle and mature art of Narayan and Joshi that save these successful characters who learn to fail gloriously and that without being self-conscious.

The Great Shashi Tharoor Show

MOHAN RAMANAN

Reading *Show Business*, Shashi Tharoor's recently reissued novel first published in 1991, left me with a sense of irritated frustration. Here is a writer of undoubted skills and enormous talent frittering away his energies on trivialities. *The Great Indian Novel* made me suspect this much but now I am confirmed in my view that Tharoor is merely a clever writer, playing to the gallery, a gallery made up of a small English educated elite which cocks its snook up at things Indian. Tharoor is not a 'serious' novelist, he is an artful one, but artful dodging takes you only thus far and no further. *The Great Indian Novel* at least was an allegory of modern India and did not go down well. It had at least one lesson to teach, that the only truth to hold fast to is that there is no absolute truth, that India is a land of pluralistic truth and experiences. In a climate of religious fundamentalism and attempts to reduce the complexity of India to a few narrow religious principles, Tharoor's message, if indeed it was seriously meant, was welcome. But even *The Great Indian Novel* is overwritten and Tharoor takes over four hundred pages to tell us this. Of course that book is entertaining and at times downright funny but even here, somewhere midway, the allegory is a bit thin and the use to which the *Mahabharata*, India's great epic, is put, is less than satisfactory.

Show Business is a shorter effort but still long enough and it is built on thin air; Bombay film world is its focus. The celluloid city is famous for what is called Bollywood. Cinema is big business and this tinsel town is well-known for its big spending, its creation of huge illusions, its escapist entertainment and its yellow journalism, scandals and hypocrisy. Tharoor chooses to satirize this world.

The novel about Bollywood's superstar Ashok Banjara, hero of *Godambo, Judai, Dil Ek Qila, Mechanic* and his last movie *Kalki*. Ashok is critically ill, fighting for his life in the intensive care unit of one of Bombay's poshest hotels—oops, I am sorry, hospitals! He is able to relive his career for us and his reverie is the main narration. Interspersed with this are the voices of his visitors—Pranay, Ashok's long time cinema villain, but in actual life, a somewhat nice man, who is in love with Ashok's wife and who has fathered an illegitimate child by her—a fact Ashok is aware of; Kulbhushan, Ashok's politician father, who is disappointed that Ashok first went into films and then that he joined politics which turned out to be a disaster; Mehnaz Elahi, Ashok's heroine in several movies, and his lover but for whom Ashok hardly has any feelings; Ashwin, Ashok's brother, who has been a grassroot political worker and who finds his patrimony—the parliamentary seat held by his father—snatched away by Ashok, but who nevertheless campaigns for his brother; and several 'voices,' all of whom give us insights into Ashok's life and career.

From these various points of view we gather that Ashok, the son of an influential politician Kulbhushan, has been promoted by a businessman-producer, Jagannath Choubey, who hopes to get Government concessions by helping Ashok. In the event Ashok whose acting talents are not too good becomes the star of *Godambo* and very soon superstar of Bollywood. The novel also takes us to the film sets of each one of the Ashok starrers and we gather that *Godambo* is the story of how Ashok, a patriotic policeman, brings to book Godambo the smuggler, played by Pranay, with the help of Abha, played by Abha, "yesterday's hearthrob" but now old enough to be Ashok's mother and just about beginning to show it. In reel-life Abha has the "famous bust out-thrust," but in real life when Ashok seduces her he realizes in horror and disbelief that her "breasts [are] so shrivelled and empty [that] they are like pockets of desiccated skin, their tips drooping in dry dismay." Nothing in Bollywood is what it seems. Everything is makebelieve.

In *Judai* (separation) Abha plays mother to Ashok who plays a double role—one as an inspector, the other as a slum hero and monkeyman (i.e. getting a monkey to play tricks). Between them they make mincement of the Thakur or landlord, played by Pranay, who has been guilty of sending their innocent father to prison and of separating the brothers. The feminine interest in the movie is Mehnaz Elahi who falls in love with Inspector Ashok, and monkey-man Ashok brings them together, after a grand reconciliation of the family and the destruction of the villains.

Other movie scripts are described and we can skip them but note in passing that *Dil Ek Qila* (The Heart is a Fortress) is a witty adaptation of the Hindi film classic Dil Ek Mandir (The Heart is a Temple). Ashok is now a politician and Tharoor is, of course, reminding us of the great Indian contemporary fact that film stars have turned politicians—the names of MGR (M.G. Ramachandran, the Tamil film hero who became Chief Minister of Tamilnadu) and NTR (N.T. Rama Rao, the Telugu film hero, who became Chief Minister of Andhra Pradesh) are repeatedly mentioned to place Ashok's film career and political aspirations in perspective. But politics leaves Ashok frustrated. He is only an ineffective back-bencher. Soon the party bosses use him to stash away funds in his Swiss-bank account and this is exposed leading to his resigning from politics. Here too Tharoor is alluding to the famous Bofors case and related financial scandals where Indian politicians and Indian actors were involved. Ashok's return to films is low key. No producer wants to support him but one producer of mythological movies takes him on for *Kalki*. Ashok plays the lead role of the avatar of Lord Vishnu who comes down to earth to redeem it from sin and corruption. But corruption-ridden Ashok has a major accident and is now fighting for his life, and *Kalki* remains unfinished.

This is the story, at times entertaining, and usually funny, but after a while it all gets tedious and one wonders what the point of it all is. Why expend so much ink over so little? Wittily Tharoor dedicates the book to his sisters, Shobha and Sunita, "in fulfilment of a twenty-year-old promise to take them to the movies." This he does by escorting us through six movie takes and skilfully weaving his narrative with multiple voices through them. We take the point that illusion is reality and reality is illusion (Ashok's demure wife is significantly named Maya (illusion) but she turns out to be unfaithful. Ashok is no Kalki because he is unredeemed in his corruption. The cinema villain is different in life, but Pranay is taking his cinematic revenge on Ashok by carrying on with Maya. Politics is like films—a tissue of lies. Cinema is politicized and there is no innocence. To say this Tharoor takes 307 pages. It was not necessary. One final comment. Tharoor's writing is part of a fictional culture in India where clever writing seems to be the order of the day. There is money in it; witness Vikram Seth's huge profits. There is fame in it, but ultimately it is all show and we feel cheated. Fiction must be made of sterner stuff.

Firdaus Kanga's *Trying to Grow* as a *Bildungsroman*

V.L.V.N. NARENDERA KUMAR

Firdaus Kanga's *Trying to Grow* is a *Bildungsroman* or a novel of education. The narrative centrestages the maturation of Brit, the protagonist and his development of an awareness of his place in the world. Brit is an imginative invalid who passionately tries to grow. The novel is autobiographical and derives its essence from the strength of the novelist's conviction that it is very rewarding to be considered ordinary. Brit's struggle in the novel is to reach the plenitude of his being. The archetypal conflict in Zoroastrianism is internalized in Brit's passage to adulthood.

Brit Kotwal is a dwarf, born afflicted with *osteogenesis imperfecta*, who is endowed with comic imagination. His parents are consummate Anglophiles in whose smug existence the hangover of colonialism still persists. In their cosy world, there is no room for religion. Brit observes thus: "We Parsees do not take our religion too seriously; those who do are considered downright dangerous and a little mad." (14)

Sera's eroticism and Sam's romanticism make him plunge into life with giddy exhilaration. Broken in body, he needs to be alive in spirit. He creates a mythical world of his own and the fairy tales and fantasies whet his appetite. He lives like a toy Prince in a toy world. Sam's scepticism and apprehensiveness, on the other hand, stem from his heightened awareness of Brit's quandary. He observes thus one day: "I don't want you to escape from what you are. It's no use pretending, if you are pretending that every thing's alright. Becuase it is n't." (37)

Brit envisages the travails and the trauma of growing up in the face of crippling circumstances. One of the triumphs of Kanga is that he does not sentimentalize the predicament of his protagonist. This is due to the detached stance he strikes.

Madame Manekshaw, a quintessential Parsee, serves as the nexus between Brit's self-built world of myths and the ever-impinging world of experience. Her perceptions are firmly rooted in the Zoroastrian ethos. It is she who initiates the process of Brit's self-development. Her perspectives are refreshingly original and insightful. Referring to Brit's obsession with literature, she remarks thus: "It's what you learn that counts, not what you study." (57) The didactic undercurrent in her pedagogy acts as a stimulant in the blossoming of his sensibilities. He, who, till then, looks at life through the spectacles of literature, realizes the futility of such an exercise.

The exclusiveness of the Zoroastrians with regard to aliens should be seen in the right perspective. Conservative Parsees have a dislike for mixed marriages. They believe that preservation of their blood from getting mixed with that of other races is an existential necessity. Freddie in Bapsi Sidhwa's *The Crow Eaters* stands between his son and Rosy Watson, a fallen Anglo-Indian girl. Such Parsees are apprehensive that mixed marriages would result in the loss of their racial identity or uniqueness which may lead to racial extinction. However, there is a notable change in the attitude of the Parsees in recent times. Lunacy which has resulted from in-breeding in the Zoroastrian community and dearth of suitable boys and girls in the community are forcing Parsees to opt for mixed marriages. This problem is dealt with in Karanjia's *More of an Indian*. What Karanjia advocates is a synthesis, a fusion of the Hindu and the Zoroastrian cultures. The narrative is an effective fictional rendering of a progressive Zoroastrian vision.

Brit's sister resolves to marry a Muslim. Her decision sets the cat among the pigeons. Like most conservative Parsees, Sam and Sera are against mixed marriages. Brit confesses thus: "When life came to solid things like marriage, everyone, even Sera and Sam, forgot how modern they are." (88) Sera regards it as a 'shameful act of betrayal.' Muslims are the traditional enemies of Parsees. Hence her rejection of her daughter's proposition. This new-found truth disturbs Brit.

Brit's tragic quandary is viewed by his parents from diametrically opposite points of view. In Sam's mind lurks an apprehension that his son would not be able to vie with young men 'bursting with energy.' Sera's optimism, on the other hand, is Browningsque. It is she who blocks Brit's encounter with reality. Her over-indulgence stunts his growth.

Brit's life acquires a new meaning after the tempestuous advent of Cyrus, son of Defarge's cousin. He treats Brit as an individual, a propensity not witnessed hitherto in his life. Cyrus's perceptions of reality are sharper than Brit's. His rejection of poetry which is Platonic in its intensity, shatters the self-built myth of Brit. Enlightening him, Cyrus observes thus once: "You know what poets do? They drag their feelings up a hill and let you go. What you read is the crash." (109)

Brit's attempt at self-assertion fails to evoke a sympathetic response in his parents. The last thing he expects from them is sympathy. Sam's realization that Brit's journey to adulthood would never be smooth and easy augments his misery. He is apprehensive that books and bridge would take his son away from the real world and the resultant divorce would lead to mental staticity.

Cyrus, on the other hand, plays the role of a catalyst in the evolution of Brit's consciousness. They become partners in the 'serious business of living.' Cyrus' past becomes the key for Brit to unlock his present. Cyrus employs music as a means to drown his anger and to alienate himself from the world. It is like building one's body at the cost of one's brain. Brit's proclivity towards homosexual life is construed as the result of a perversion by Sera wheras Sam feigns indifference.

There is a tinge of irony in Brit's resolve to become a creative writer. This activity, which involves his self, enables him to conquer loneliness. The publication of his story and the ensuing success inspire him. He observes: "But I got something bigger from that story. I didn't feel alone anymore. How could I? I had just talked to fifty thousand people." (155)

Brit's success dispels Sam's notion of defeatism. His ennui in the fragile glass world is fructifying. He resolves to end his self-imposed exile. He tells Ruby once: "Yes, I've lived inside a paper crystal paperweight and now I want to know the real world, other people, people who are not like me." (158) However, the spell cast by literature is so profound that he continues to dwell in the west, mentally and emotionally. He is reminded of Naples (a place he never visited), when he has at his feet, Bombay, 'a proud city with so much life it burns into the night.' His failure to 'connect' the ideal and the real is due to his 'imprisoned imagination.'

The dramatic death of Sam fills Brit with awe. His father, a romantic through and through, makes several mad bids for freedom. His attempt to cross the road blindfolded is his 'last classy act.' He looks at life too straight, loves his family too much and hopes too much. He is a failed quester and the aeroplanes he loves are symbols of freedom. It is a moment of loss but it is also the juncture where Brit stands exposed to life. He admits thus: "I felt as if all my life I'd been bundled up against the wind and now one by one, my woolies were being taken from me." (169) Gradually, the gap between his immature past and fluid present is bridged. The metamorphosis of Brit is due, to a large extent, to Amy's 'unconscious benevolence.'

Brit's first confrontation with *Druj* (Evil) occurs when he encounters his drunken servant. it is an acid test of his strength of mind. After the 'brave act,' he reflects: "Like Hitler or someone who felt so awful about themselves, so weak, so powerless, the only way they could feel alright was by making someone else feel that way." (181)

The day in shadow ends with Brit's realization that he is no longer a boy with osteo but a man. After Amy's rescue act at the theatre, he accepts his limitations with humility. His reflection in the mirror sickens him. It is not what he wants to perceive but what he wishes to eschew. It is a tryst with truth. His success as a writer gives him an identity. His mother's absurd and comic death does not leave a void behind. Speaking of his options, he says boldly thus: "I want to be what I really am, no more acts, no more reaching for things I'm too short to reach." (233) Like Joyce's Stephen, he steps into the 'real' world with hope. From an Edenic state of pristine innocence, Brit progresses to a level of awareness, a point from which he views the human comedy with comic-ironic detachment. In the narrative, there is a conscious progression from confusion, born of innocence and inaction, to decisiveness and action, which spring from a heightened consciousness. The shift of his mind is from a *tamasic* state to a *rajasic* one. His recognition of his role in the world becomes the culminating point of the growth of his consciousness in the narrative. In a nutshell, the shift of Brit's mind is from *Angra Mainyu* (Lower Mind) to *Spenta Mainyu* (Higher Mind).

Trying to Grow bears the stamp of intimate personal experience. In the novel, the autobiographical facts are fused with the elements of fictionality. The fusion is so subtle that it is well nigh impossible to distinguish between Kanga, the creator, and Brit, the creation. Kanga's first creative effort, written with compelling honesty, offers a rich slice of Zoroastrian life. Brit's efforts to escape from an intellectually sterile ambience, to discover his true self constitute the core of the novel. It is a noteworthy work in Parsee fiction in English, for it tells us much about the disintegration of the Zoroastrian community in the post-colonial context.

NOTE

1. Firdaus Kanga, *Trying to Grow* (New Delhi: Ravi Dayal, 1990).

Indo-Anglian Critical Scene: Notes towards a Perspective

S. KRISHNA SARMA

A critic starts with the conviction that his approach to his subject is quite unbiased and that he owes it to his reading public to say what he believes as true about a book or an author. If he is not convinced about his infallibility, he would not set down his opinions. Again, it is true that a critic is responsible to his reading public. But he owes a responsibility to the book or the author as well, in that he should try his modest best to be objective, for, notwithstanding what one may say about 'personal heresy' it is unnatural for a critic not to be guided and controlled by his mental culture and critical sensibility.

When a critic attempts an evaluation of an ancient book or a book from another country, he faces a complex problem. Not only should he evaluate the book in terms of its local or contemporaneous set of values, but also guage its relevance to his time and to his country. He cannot hold one scale of values for ancient writings and a different, more lenient, scale for modern writings; and again, he cannot have a more austere scale of values for books coming from another country and an easier scale for those of his own country. Yet, there are many who swear by old literary values and dismiss modern writing as non-artistic, and there are those also who dismiss all old writings as 'Victorian.' Similarly, there are some critics who swear by British critical values, and dismiss English writing from outside as 'overseas' writing and therefore second rate. There are also not wanting critics who would condescend to appreciate this 'overseas' writing and eulogize either on the ground—similar to the attitude of some British and American Professors who pass a mediocre doctoral dissertation from India that it is "good enough for them" or that "you can't expect anything better from them," or on the ground that the books are exotic, topographically informative and sociologically educative.

Having two different scales of evaluation is hypocritical, and is a symptom of unsound critical sensibility. On the other hand, having a monolithic attitude indicates intolerance and bigotry, and is equally bad for literary criticism. But to appear to have a single scale of values and use it out of smugness or for wrong reasons is far more dangerous, because it is unethical.

There is yet another temptation, for the critic: it is parochialism, what George Woodcock calls, "literary incestuousness." One praises an author because he belongs to one's region, or one's village: "We must help our own people," or "if we ignore our men, who else will praise them?" attitude; and on the other hand, one praises another writer because the other had praised the former one—"you scratch my back, and I shall scratch yours" attitude. Both these attitudes are symptoms of a critical sensibility which is diseased.

For all these ills, the only remedy seems to be 'objectivity' not of the monolithic, formalist kind, but a sympathetic application of one set of literary values as guidelines for evaluating a book. One might even term it as "enlightened subjectivity," since the critic attempts to translate his response to a book in terms of its artistic achievement but also necessarily takes into consideration the writer's values, local or contemporaneous situation, the writer's intentions as well as the final achievement. All this is done in terms of the all-pervasive criteria of harmony, beauty and goodness.

Under these conditions, the position of an Indo-Anglian critic is quite unenviable. He is surrounded by parochialists, the regional literary critics (vernacularists) who despise the foreign foliation, and the purists who try to out-British the British critics and maintain that Indo-Anglian literature at its best is an extension, rather than an anaemic one, of English literature, and at its worst, it is but scrappy journalism. The Indo-Anglian critic cannot emulate the purist: then the best native writing would appear as minor Shakespeare, pseudo-Keats, second-rate Tennyson, third-rate Eliot, local Hardy or Indian Scott etc: it would be self-defeating, and would hardly be fair to the native poet or novelist. Nor can he emulate the regionalist: then the entire Indo-Anglian literature would be balkanised: admire Kamala Markandaya because she hails from Karnataka, Khushwant Singh because he is a Sikh, and so on. It is like a Bengali critic praising Bengali poetry, and a Tamil critic maintaining that Tamil writing is the source of all culture, and so on. Such attitudes do not have critical validity, at best in the area of Indo-Anglian writing.

The Indo-Anglian critic should steer clear of these two perils, the Scylla and Charybdis, for easy sailing. His is a rich legacy of classical sensibility, enriched—and not vitiated—by his exposure to the western and particularly British, literary sensibility. He should therefore be more sympathetic and understanding and less bigotted. But that should not make criticism an apology for cherishing and fostering second-rate writing. On the contrary, the critic, aware of the perennial values which make a book a work of art, should see the extent of modification in a particular book, find an explanation for it if possible, pick out the best the author has to offer in the book, and should see if it contributes to greater human understanding; or dismiss it only if there is nothing redeeming in the book, not on the ground that it was not written by a Kalidasa, a Homer, a Milton, or a Keats. Such critical task requires a deeper sympathy and greater large-heartedness than is usually possessed by a critic who undertakes to 'criticize.'

Let us look at some of the critical attitudes currently in vogue in Indo-Anglian literature. There is the amusing controversy about the term 'Indo-Anglian' popularized by Srinivasa Iyengar to describe this literature. People in academic circles have come to feel now that the term is not elegant enough. So they replace it with the half-caste 'Indo-English' or the circuitous 'Indian writing in English.' The latter is no doubt descriptive, and Iyengar himself has used it as a title for his book surveying the Indian creative writing in English. But you cannot form an adjective out of it: you cannot, for instance, refer to Narayan as 'Indian writing in English Novelist' or 'Indian novelist in English' etc. On the other hand, 'Indo-Anglian' lends itself beautifully to adjectival usage with ease and without alteration.

I called the term 'Indo-English' half-caste because, in addition to its phonetic infelicity, the term is unbalanced: the second part attracts the main stress to itself so that a phrase like 'Indo-English novelist' would almost indicate an English novelist of an Indian brand. Both in sense and balance 'Indo-Anglian' is as felicitous as 'French Canadian'; yet some of our critics and academicians shy away from the phrase simply because some reputed Professor somewhere had shown aversion to it.

For another example, take the critical controversy surrounding the writings of Nirad Chaudhuri. The Indo-Anglian critic is so shocked by the views and opinions of Mr. Chaudhuri that he fails to see that the writer was trying to do precisely that—shock the reader and criticize. The critic hurriedly brands Mr. Chaudhuri an 'Anglophile' as though that would explain everything about his art, his love for Indian culture, his love of human dignity and human wellbeing. The critic allows himself to be drawn into a personal quarrel with the writer, as if the criticism were directed against him personally. The writer may be largely responsible for this kind of critical reaction; he loves to shock and to make controversial statements. It may be felt that Mr. Chaudhuri has twisted history to suit his arguments. But then, rather than resent it, the critic should find out why such a keen student of history and civilization as Mr. Chaudhuri has done so. A little consideration is likely to show that he was merely overdoing it, and getting carried away in his enthusiasm. This imbalance in attitude is one of the faults which the critic should not hasten to condemn. He should find out why Mr. Chaudhuri allows this imbalance to taint his creative process, and allows the so-called 'Anglophilism' to creep into his works. It would not be too difficult to see that Mr. Chaudhuri's anti-Indian stance is not through 'hatred' so much as a protest against the absence of some basic values which should be there in any society worth the name.

The case of Nirad Chaudhuri is perhaps an extreme example, but similar things are happening in the fields of poetry and fiction. For instance, the reaction against Tagore and Aurobindo on the ground that one is sentimentalist and the other obscurantist. Though this revolt is limited to a small section of the critical community, its presence itself is a symptom of a critical malaise.

The Indo-Anglian critic should be less eager to strike, should be more generous, and be a more authentic *sahridaya*. There is one critic amongst us who exemplifies the special qualities of an Indo-Anglian critic, Srinivasa Iyengar. He has no doubt been a pioneer in this field, and a remarkable one too. In some quarters it has been felt that since his evaluations have been largely of a pioneering nature and mostly biography-oriented, others should take over the task of assessing the achievements of the Indo-Anglian writers, now we find a series of evaluations, assessments and reassessments of writers, big and small—it is enough if a poet or poetaster has brought out a single volume of verse, enough if one has published a novel: they would merit a book of critical evaluation. It is indeed doubtful to what extent many of such critical evaluations in the 'Indian writers and their work' series are basically different from, or show any marked improvement upon Srinivasa Iyengar's *Indian Writing in English*.

But look at the critical temperament which pervades *Indian Writing in English*: genial understanding, exploratory, as well as evaluative. The chapters on Sarojini Naidu, Tagore, Sri Aurobindo, the great novelists, to name a few, are so balanced and so excitingly seminal. There is an attempt to see the writer from all sides and to discover the source of his/her artistic strength to bring out in a fair measure the best in the artist, and no eagerness to 'criticize' and yet the critic never really loses sight of the ultimate in literary appreciation. This generosity, all-comprehensiveness, this fine sense of discrimination and this critical fairplay are such a precious ware that an Indo-Anglian critic of the present generation would do well to emulate these qualities till he attains a maturer critical sensibility.

Appendix

The Post-Graduate Department of English, Andhra Loyola College, Vijayawada conducted a seminar on Indian Writing in English in February 1996. Post-Graduate students from colleges affiliated to Nagarjuna University participated in the seminar. Prof. K. Venkata Reddy, Dept. of English, Sri Krishnadevaraya University, Anantapur, delivered the keysnote address. He made a comprehensive assessment of pre-Independence writers like Venkataramani, Tagore, Sarojini Naidu and Sri Aurobindo. He examined, though briefly, epoch-making works like *Untouchable*. He discussed the works of Indian playwrights like Karnad, Badal Sircar and Vijay Tendulkar. He dismissed the apprehensions of detractors like the Canada-based Uma Parameswaran. Referring to the use of English by the Indian creative writers, Prof. Reddy quoted Kamala Das. Indian literature is being enriched by the contributions of promising writers like Amitav Ghosh, Gita Mehta and others. Prof. Reddy ended his address on an optimistic note saying that Indian writing would grow and establish itself as a major literature in the world.

In all, nine papers were presented on different genres of Indian writing in English. Mrs. Vishnu Vandana of Maris Stella College, discussed the treatment of love-theme in Sarojini Naidu's "The Temple." Miss Himabala, an undergraduate student from St. Theresa's College, Eluru, read a paper on the use of narrative technique in Karnad's *Hayavadana*. Miss Lavanya from the same college presented a paper on Kamala Das. Two students from University College, Nagarjuna University, Mr. Rajeswara Rao and Miss Rohini, read papers on Narayan and Raja Rao respectively.

Three Post-Graduate students of Andhra Loyola College participated in the seminar. Mr. Sunny Jacob read a paper on Anantamurthy's *Samskara* which generated an interesting discussion. Mr. Sanjeev Kumar in his paper on Anita Desai's *Cry, the Peacock* examined the predicament of Maya. Miss Sreedevi's paper was on Dina Mehta's award-winning play *The Brides Are Not for Burning*. This paper was read out at the seminar by Miss Meghana.

The Post-Graduate students responded enthusiastically to this stimulating event. It was a literary event with a difference in which there was not a single dull moment.

Contributors

G. S. Balarama Gupta is a distinguished critic of Indian literature in English. He is the author of *Mulk Raj Anand*. He edits *The Journal of Indian Writing in English*. At present, he is the Head and Chairman, Department of English, Gulbarga University, Gulbarga.

V.L.V.N. Narendra Kumar is the author of *Fits and Misfits: A Study of Anita Desai's Protagonists*. His research articles have appeared in some Indian journals. He teaches at the Post-Graduate Dept. of English, Andhra Loyola College, Vijayawada.

E. Manickam teaches at I.I.T., Madras.

Prema Nandakumar is a widely published critic and reviewer. One of the leading authorities on Indian writing in English today, her publications include *Sri Aurobindo*, *A Study of 'Savitri'* and *Atom and the Serpent,* a novel on campus life in India.

M. Rajagopalachary is the author of two monographs, the first on the fiction of Manohar Malgonkar and the second on Bernard Malamud. He teaches at the Dept. of English, Kakatiya University Post-Graduate Centre, Nirmal.

M. Rajeshwar has published numerous articles and a full-length study, *The Novels of Wole Soyinka.* Currently, he is the Associate Editor of *Kakatiya Journal of English Studies*. He teaches at the Dept. of English, Kakatiya University, Warangal.

Ragini Ramachandra has published numerous articles and reviews. She teaches in a college affiliated to Bangalore University.

Mohan Ramanan is a reputed scholar whose interests are varied. His papers have appeared in many journals, Indian and international. He is Professor of English at Central University of Hyderabad.

V. Rangan has contributed numerous scholarly articles to journals and periodicals. He is the author of a monograph on John Synge. He retired as Professor of English, Nagarjuna University, Nagarjuna Nagar.

P. Hari Padma Rani is a budding scholar. She took an M.Phil. in ELT from University of Hyderabad. She teaches at Andhra Pradesh Residential Junior College, Nagarjuna Sagar.

T. Ashoka Rani is a frequently published scholar who is keenly interested in women's studies. Currently, she is Head, Dept. of English, Sri Padmavathi Mahila Viswavidyalayam, Tirupati.

Ranga Rao is the author of *Fowl-Filcher*. He teaches at Sri Venkateswara College, New Delhi.

Latha Rengachari is a young researcher in the Dept. of Humanities, I.I.T., Madras. She is writing her Ph.D. thesis on Third World Women Novelists.

K. Sampath is a research scholar in the Dept of English, Kakatiya University, Warangal.

E. Satyanarayana is a young scholar who wrote his doctoral thesis on Mahasweta Devi's plays. He contributed a few papers to anthologies. He teaches at University Art & Science College, Kakatiya University, Warangal.

S. Krishna Sharma is the author of *Imagery in the Plays of Christopher Fry, The Achievement of Christopher Fry and Other Essays* and *Seed of Grandeur*. He has contributed scholarly articles and reviews to several journals and periodicals. He retired as Professor of English, Nagarjuna University, Nagarjuna Nagar.

Ravi Nandan Sinha has published poetry and criticism in India, Pakistan, USA, Canada and Korea. His work has also been anthologised. He received the International Writers Award, University of Colorado, USA. For almost a decade now, he has been editing *The Quest*, a journal of Indian Writing in English read in over fifteen countries. Presently, he is Head, Dept. of English, St Xavier's College, Ranchi, Bihar.

Mrinalini Solanki teaches English at Women's Polytechnic College, Jodhpur, Rajasthan.

C.N. Srinath is a well known critic of Commonwealth literature. His publications include *The Literary Landscape, The Flowering of Australian Literature* and *Glimpses of Canadian Literature*. He is the Editor of *The Literary Criterion*. He teaches at the Dept. of English, Bangalore University, Bangalore.

Index